THE STEPS OF A
GOOD
MAN

EMBRACING THE COMMITMENTS
OF GODLY MANHOOD

ELDON MARTENS

First published in 2008 by Striving Together Publications, a ministry of Lancaster Baptist Church, Lancaster, CA 93535. Striving Together Publications is committed to providing tried, trusted, and proven books that will further equip local churches to carry out the Great Commission. Your comments and suggestions are valued.

Striving Together Publications
4020 E. Lancaster Blvd.
Lancaster, CA 93535
800.201.7748

Cover design by Andrew Jones
Layout by Sarah Michael and Craig Parker
Edited by Cary Schmidt and Sarah Michael
Special thanks to our proofreaders

ISBN 978-1-59894-048-0

Printed in the United States of America

DEDICATION

For years a number of individuals have encouraged me
to do some writing, as there is certainly a great need
for sound material for men from fundamental Baptist
churches. My strongest cheerleader and supporter has
been Martha, my precious wife of forty-four years. Because
of her encouragement and assistance, this book has
become a reality. I am indebted for her hours of typing the
manuscript and the editing, correcting and laboring at my
side. No greater gift has been given to me outside of my
salvation than my friend, Martha.

Table of Contents

FOREWORD

The *Steps of a Good Man* was written by a man whose steps have been Christ-pleasing in his marriage and ministry. For nearly four decades the name Eldon Martens has been one that always stood for soulwinning zeal and integrity. I have watched Dr. Martens as his steps have taken him away from friends who walked into compromise, and toward cities that needed a new church that would preach the Gospel of Jesus Christ. I have observed as his steps led toward developing a godly marriage and family, and I have watched him walk faithfully through times of trial.

Perhaps one of the times when pastors in the West most respected Dr. Eldon Martens was during a time—for reasons known only to God—he completely lost his voice. For a preacher to lose his voice is something like a major league baseball player losing both arms. Dr. Martens literally could not do the thing God had called him to do!

During that time, I watched the steps of this good man as he took various forms of secular work to provide for his family. He never stopped praying; he never stopped trusting; and he never stopped walking for the Lord. What a great day it was when God restored his voice and allowed him to begin pastoring again!

In short, you are not reading a book written by a man who hopes he will walk in the ways of God. It is a book written by a man who has been down the path and wants to help you realize that by following Christ's pattern, you too may become a man of integrity.

We are pleased that Striving Together Publications can join with this good man and follow along that same path of Christian living with him.

May God bless and enrich you as you apply these biblical principles to your life.

Dr. Paul Chappell
April 2008

INTRODUCTION

Throughout forty years of ministry I have watched, with great disappointment, Christian men with a lack of spiritual character and fortitude. As a result, these men (with good hearts) have found their lives, their marriages, and their children defeated and in disarray. How do so many of God's men get to this point in life? How do men—who know the living God, who understand (in their minds) the truths of Scripture, and who (to a measure) comprehend the power of the living God at their disposal—find themselves in spiritual defeat?

The answer is that good men become *hearers* of the Word and fail to be *doers* of the Word. This is what "separates the men from the boys" spiritually speaking. James 1:22 states, *"But be ye doers of the word, and not hearers only, deceiving your own selves."* As an old adage says, "You can lead a horse to water, but you can't make him drink." There must come a time in a man's life when he determines to live out the truths he has heard—when he decides to take action personally. He must yield to the Word and the will of God and then live out these truths by the power of the Holy Spirit.

I am reminded of the passage found in Psalm 37:23 where David states, *"The steps of a good man are ordered* (literally prepared) *by the LORD: and he delighteth in his way."* The path and steps before us have already been laid out, and all we must do is follow. We all have a decision, to follow His way or to go our own way. The psalmist said, *"I have chosen the way of truth..."* (Psalm 119:30). May it be each man's choice to follow in His steps and to find His path our delight.

Several years ago, the Lord began to burden my heart to conduct a meeting that would challenge men to embrace God's call to godliness. In response to this burden, I scheduled a meeting with all the independent, fundamental Baptist pastors in the area, in which I told the men that I would organize such a conference if they would get behind me and support it. They all consented, and I began to pray and consider how the Lord would have me move forward.

I was encouraged to contact Pastor Dave Teis at Liberty Baptist Church in Las Vegas, Nevada, who had conducted a similar meeting. After conversing with Pastor Teis, he gave me permission to use the name "Master's Men" and shared some basic ideas for me to consider. Our desire was to have an old-fashioned men's revival meeting with preaching as the centerpiece. Since 1995, we have conducted this annual revival for men and young men with God's blessing and unusual growth—from 170 in attendance the first year to over 1,000 in attendance.

This book is the outgrowth of the Master's Men's conferences, in which we have promoted the "Nine Commitments of a Master's Man." I wanted to place into the hands of Christian men a tool the Lord might use to help men live out these nine biblical commitments.

I trust that as you read through this short book and then do the three "action steps" at the end of each chapter, you will become a growing, godly man. We need men with hearts for God and a willingness to be all that they should be for Him, for their wives and children, and for their pastors. Please let me know if this book has been a blessing and a help to you. You can email me at docmart@juno.com.

Yours for the Master's Men,
Dr. Eldon Martens

PART ONE

The Heart of a
Good Man

CHAPTER ONE

Having a Genuine Heart for God

The greatest need of any man is to know God and walk with the Almighty in a real, genuine, and personal relationship. The great tragedy, however, is that many men who profess to know this awesome God have never entered into a real relationship with Him through faith in the Lord Jesus Christ. A man cannot have a genuine heart for God until he has been redeemed and rescued by God's grace through faith in Christ.

There are those men, who are *professors* of salvation, but they are not *possessors*, and in that revealing moment as these professors stand before the Judge of all the ages, they will profess "...*Lord, Lord, have we not prophesied in thy name? and in thy name have we cast out devils? and in thy name done many wonderful works?*" And then the Lord Himself will declare those harrowing words, "...*I never knew you: depart from me, ye that work iniquity*" (Matthew 7:22–23).

Salvation is in a Person, and that Person is the Lord Jesus Christ. "*But as many as received him, to them gave he power to become the sons of God, even to them that believe on his name"* (John 1:12). The Gospel message revolves around the death, burial, and resurrection of Christ in that He fully propitiated (satisfied) the wrath of Almighty God by His redeeming work on the Cross of Calvary for our sins. We must come to Christ, recognize our wicked and wretched condition, and cast ourselves upon His mercy, *"Not by works of righteousness which we have done, but according to his mercy he saved us, by the washing of regeneration, and renewing of the Holy Ghost"* (Titus 3:5).

It is by simple repentance and faith in Christ that we are saved. *"Testifying both to the Jews, and also to the Greeks, repentance toward God, and faith toward our Lord Jesus Christ"* (Acts 20:21). If you have never settled this most vital matter, right now, bow your head, open your heart, and cry out to God, simply trusting in Christ and Him alone to save you.

You might consider using this simple prayer:

"Dear God, I come to You right now as a helpless, hell-bound sinner, recognizing my hopeless condition, and I ask for Your full forgiveness. Lord Jesus, right now I am trusting in your sacrifice for me on the Cross, as You shed Your blood and paid for my sins and rose again from the dead. I now receive you as my personal Saviour. Thank You for saving me today. Amen."

Once a man has fully settled this key issue, he can experience and enjoy a wonderful relationship with the living God and an ongoing heart for God.

Having a genuine heart for God and enjoying daily personal revival should be the norm for a godly man. *Revival* simply means "to live again." It is the work God does in our lives as we come to Him as believers and humbly empty ourselves of sin, rebellion, and disobedience by confessing and forsaking those things that have robbed us of revival. *"If we confess our sins, he is faithful and just to forgive us our sins, and to cleanse us from all unrighteousness"* (1 John 1:9).

A man who truly wants a heart for God can experience this wonderful, personal revival, and it all begins with a desire to seek after Him. *"But if from thence thou shalt seek the LORD thy God, thou shalt find him, if thou seek him with all thy heart and with all thy soul"* (Deuteronomy 4:29).

The Lord hungers for fellowship with us, and He is looking for any man whose heart is turned toward Him. *"For the eyes of the LORD run to and fro throughout the whole earth, to shew himself strong in the behalf of them whose heart is perfect toward him..."* (2 Chronicles 16:9).

Physically, the human heart is an amazing creation of God. The heart is a hard-working marvel that can continue beating automatically even if all nerves are severed! It beats an average of seventy-five times a minute, forty million times a year, and two-and-a-half billion times by the time a person is seventy years old. With each beat, the average adult heart pumps four ounces of blood. This amounts to three thousand gallons a day and over one million gallons a year. The heart produces enough energy in a twelve hour period to lift a sixty-five-ton railroad car in the air.

The heart is an organ that is absolutely necessary for life. Many people die every year because of heart disease. Many people take medication to strengthen their hearts—to control blood pressure, to reduce cholesterol, to prevent blood clots. It is absolutely vital that we take care of the "old ticker."

A Johns Hopkins University medical researcher discovered what the *Presbyterian Minister Life Insurance Company* had known for more than two centuries. "Attending church is good for your health." The risk of fatal heart disease is almost twice as high for non-church goers than for men who attend once a week or more, according to a study made by Dr. George W. Comstock of the Johns Hopkins University's Department of Epidemiology.

A healthy heart is vital for a full and enjoyable life. This is true physically, but it is also true spiritually. The spiritual heart affects the physical heart. *"A merry heart doeth good like a medicine..."* (Proverbs 17:22). We need to take care of our spiritual hearts. *"Keep* (guard) *thy heart with all diligence; for out of it are the issues of life"*

(Proverbs 4:23). God is much more concerned about our spiritual hearts than He is about our physical hearts.

As we begin this journey to study the marks of a godly man, I want you to consider truly having a heart for God. A heart for God should be your first priority if you desire a joyous, fulfilling, and fruitful life.

It has always been the heart of God to bless and prosper His people as they walk with a heart for Him. "...*For the LORD seeth not as man seeth; for man looketh on the outward appearance, but the LORD looketh on the heart*" (1 Samuel 16:7).

If we will be men fit for the Master's use, we must first be men after the Master's heart. There was only one man in the Bible who was said to be a "man after God's own heart"—David. Of all the men in the Bible, why was David chosen to bear that title? I have wondered this many times and, in studying David's life, I have found there is nothing extraordinary about him. He was just a man who surrendered his life to do what God told him to do. And as all men do, he sometimes chose his own way and paid dearly for it. The man who would truly have a genuine heart for God, as David did, will pursue some basic qualities.

We will see some of these qualities in the book of Joshua. In Joshua 22:1–6 we find that the Promised Land had been conquered. God had delivered all of the land to Israel.

> And the LORD gave unto Israel all the land which he sware to give unto their fathers; and they possessed it, and dwelt therein. And the LORD gave them rest round about, according to all that he sware unto their fathers: and there stood not a man of all their enemies before them; the LORD delivered all their enemies into their hand. There failed not ought of any good thing which the LORD had spoken unto the house of Israel; all came to pass.—JOSHUA 21:43–45

The land west of the Jordan had been conquered and divided. *"Then Joshua called the Reubenites, and the Gadites, and the half tribe of Manasseh"* (Joshua 22:1). These two-and-a-half tribes had faithfully fought at the side of their brethren for more than seven long years. They had left their loved ones on the east side of Jordan to go fight the Canaanites.

> *And said unto them, Ye have kept all that Moses the servant of the LORD commanded you, and have obeyed my voice in all that I commanded you: Ye have not left your brethren these many days unto this day, but have kept the charge of the commandment of the LORD your God. And now the LORD your God hath given rest unto your brethren, as he promised them: therefore now return ye, and get you unto your tents, and unto the land of your possession, which Moses the servant of the LORD gave you on the other side Jordan.*
> —JOSHUA 22:2–4

They endured hardships and loneliness. Now, as had been promised, they could go home. So Joshua, the commander, blessed them and sent them on their way in Joshua 22:6.

But in verse 5 there is a very vital and pointed list of spiritual commitments they were to follow if they were to have a heart for God, *"But take diligent heed to do the commandment and the law, which Moses the servant of the LORD charged you, to love the LORD your God, and to walk in all his ways, and to keep his commandments, and to cleave unto him, and to serve him with all your heart and with all your soul."* In this verse, the word *heart* refers to the "inner man" (Hebrew word *lebale*) and is often compounded with the soul, the total inner man (the seat of emotion, will, intellect, etc.). The end of the verse says, *"…with all your heart and with all your soul"* (the total inner man).

They had faithfully followed all of the military commandments, and great victories had been won—enemies had been defeated. Now Joshua shares some basic steps to these tribes about being faithful to their God as they returned to their families. If we are going to have *a heart for God* we need to take heed to the five principles that Joshua shared.

Love the Lord

The Bible commands us 250 times to "love the Lord." This is a commitment of our **affections**! The admonition is given to us in 1 John 2:15, *"Love not the world, neither the things that are in the world...."* *"Set your affection on things above, not on things on the earth"* (Colossians 3:2). What we focus upon is what we come to love. That is why many men struggle with wrong affections. Their focus is wrong! They are not focusing upon the Lord.

There is a *neglect* of the Word instead of *daily* Bible reading. There is *unfaithfulness* to God's house instead of *faithful attendance*. There is *no* meditation upon His goodness instead of *genuine focus*.

In a cold, frigid region of wintry Alberta, Canada, there is an area where there is no snow, and lush green grass grows year-round. How can that be? In 1939, an underground fire broke out in the Cadomin Mine, directly beneath that area, and the fire has never been put out! The fire is what keeps the grass growing. Second Corinthians 5:14 says, *"For the love of Christ constraineth us...."* Love is a decision—a decision to never let the fire of love for God die in my heart. As my love for the Lord grows, my understanding of His infinite love for me grows, and I grow and develop spiritually.

According to medical science, unloved babies do not grow properly. Noted pediatrician, Dr. C. G. Jenkins stated, "Nurses caring for unloved babies are taught to look at them and talk to them until babies fix their eyes upon the nurses' faces. When these babies become aware of the nurses' faces they start to gain weight and grow!

The hymn writer, Helen Lemmel, stated, "Turn your eyes upon Jesus, look full in His wonderful face and the things of earth will grow strangely dim…." As you focus upon Jesus, your love for Him grows, and your understanding of His love increases. The result is that you will grow and develop a deeper *heart for God*.

Walk in All His Ways

This is a commitment of *direction*. Determine, by faith, to go in God's direction. Don't just make decisions and say, "I sure hope the Lord is going my way!" Find out which way the Lord is going and head in that direction! *"Trust in the LORD with all thine heart; and lean not unto thine own understanding. In all thy ways acknowledge him, and he shall direct thy paths"* (Proverbs 3:5–6). Go with God and He will go with you!

In life, we often make decisions without consulting the Lord or seeking His will. I love the testimony of Enoch in Genesis 5:22, *"And Enoch walked with God after he begat Methuselah three hundred years…."* Step by step, choose to walk in the same direction as the Lord. In Psalm 56:13 David said, *"…that I may walk before God in the light of the living."* Psalm 119:45 says, *"And I will walk at liberty: for I seek thy precepts."* This applies to the decisions of life. The Word of God reveals the will of God for our lives. Psalm 119:105 says, *"Thy Word is a lamp unto my feet, and a light unto my path."* Make a deliberate choice to seek, to know, and to follow the Lord in the direction He wants you to go.

Keep His Commandments

This is a step of *submission*. The greatest struggle we face does not come from this world or from Satan's attacks; our greatest struggle is with our *flesh*—my way or God's way.

We have a choice to make—to obey what we know is right to do, or to disobey and do what our flesh wants to do. Remember

Paul's dilemma as he cried out in Romans 7:19, *"For the good that I would I do not: but the evil which I would not, that I do."* The answer to Paul's dilemma is in verse 25, *"through Jesus Christ our Lord...."* Also in Philippians 4:13, *"I can do all things through Christ which strengtheneth me."* Keeping His commandments is not grievous but victorious as we obey through His power.

Each day, throughout the day, the choice is given to us—my way (disobedience) or God's way (obedience). We choose lust or purity, forgiveness or anger, deceit or honesty. Day by day, choose to walk in obedience to God's Word with a willing spirit.

Focus on loving Him (affections), walking with Him (direction), and obeying Him (submission).

Cleave unto Him

In Hebrew, the word *cleave* means "to cling to, hold fast." This is a step of *dependence*. Second Corinthians 5:7 says, *"For we walk by faith, not by sight."* We are to depend upon God by faith, *"But without faith it is impossible to please him..."* (Hebrews 11:6).

Have you ever watched an infant learning to walk? They take baby steps holding tightly to Mommy's or Daddy's hand. After a short period of time, that child no longer wants help. As humans, we love to see ourselves as independent and self-sufficient, yet our heavenly Father wants us to depend upon Him. He expects us to depend upon His power to strengthen and sustain us.

Another use of the word *cleave* is the verb *glue*. God wants us to stick to Him like glue—to hang on, to cling. Years ago, I was on a flight up the Hudson River in a small aircraft. There was a storm which caused that plane to bounce every which way! Needless to say, I was "cleaving" to my seat!

Are you "cleaving" to God? Learn to live totally dependent upon God, and throughout the day, express your great need for the Lord through prayer.

Serve Him

Joshua says, *"...to serve him with all your heart and with all your soul"* (Joshua 22:5). This is a test of our *priorities*. The challenge is to serve (work/labor/minister) with our entire beings.

Everyone has the same amount of time in a day and in a week. Although some have fuller schedules than others, we all face a test of our priorities. What takes priority in your schedule—sleep, work, family, recreation, eating, or wasting time? Mark 10:45 says, *"...the Son of man came not to be ministered unto, but to minister...."*

Serving God is not a *position* we fill but a *priority* we follow. Serving Him is the priority of ministering to others for His glory. Often we find ourselves having no time for serving God simply because it is not a priority. Look for opportunities to serve. See yourself as the servant and His minister to encourage others—regardless of your vocation.

What are you doing to serve the Lord with all your heart and with all your soul—your total being? What if you had just one day left to live?

> **One Day to Live**
> Had I but one day to live,
> One day to love, one day to give,
> One day to work and watch and raise
> My voice to God in joyous praise,
> One day to succor those in need,
> Pour healing balm on hearts that bleed,
> Or wipe the tears from sorrow's face,
> And hearten those in sad disgrace—
> I'd spend, O God, much time with Thee
> That Thou might'st plan my day for me.
> Most earnestly I'd seek to know
> The way that Thou would'st have me go,
> For Thou alone can see the heart—
> Thou knowest man's most inward part.
> —Alice Muir

Summary

If you are to have **a heart for God** the challenge is to:

1. Love the Lord—a test of affections
2. Walk in All His Ways—a test of direction
3. Keep His Commandments—a test of submission
4. Cleave unto Him—a test of dependence
5. Serve Him—a test of priorities

Action Steps

Here are three **Action Steps** to help you develop a genuine heart for God. (Initial and date when completed.)

1. Next week, make it a daily exercise to pray, "Lord, help me to have a heart for You."

   x_____   Date_____

2. Write out Deuteronomy 4:29 on a 3 x 5 card, and memorize this verse within the next week.

   x_____   Date_____

3. Tell your wife or a friend about your desire and decision to have a genuine heart for God. Ask them to pray for you and to keep you accountable on a regular, weekly basis.

   x_____   Date_____

CHAPTER TWO

Guarding Our Hearts for Continual Revival

John 7:37–38, Ephesians 5:18

The mighty Amazon River is four thousand miles long. It is a powerful body of water flowing into the Atlantic. This powerful mass of water begins as a mere trickle from an Andes glacier, and as the Amazon winds across the torrid wilderness, hundreds of tributaries pour their waters into it, causing the Amazon to carry more water than any other river in the world. So great is the Amazon's power that even when it reaches the Atlantic, the Amazon refuses to die. It floods the ocean with its muddy waters for up to one hundred miles off shore. This amazing river begins with a mere trickle and ends over ninety-miles wide. What an amazing transformation! What makes the Amazon so great and powerful? It is the tributaries that pour their waters into the river, filling and overflowing it.

Christian, what can make a seemingly small and insignificant child of God become so strong, full, and overflowing in his Christian life? It is simply the controlling of God—the filling of the Holy Spirit in his life.

God desires to work mightily in and through us, by His Holy Spirit and through the work of revival. The subject of *revival* is very near and dear to the heart of God and to those who truly walk with Him. Psalm 85:6 states, *"Wilt thou not revive us again: that thy people may rejoice in thee?"* The word *revive* means "to live again" (new life).

God's desire and plan is for every believer to be continually filled by the Holy Spirit of God and *not* to walk in the flesh. Galatians 5:16–24 speaks of this. Verse 16 says, *"This I say then, Walk in the Spirit, and ye shall not fulfill the lust of the flesh."*

As children of God, we can and should live under the control of the Holy Spirit and experience a continual reviving in our hearts. Yet, we cannot do this filling and reviving work on our own. There must be a desire to be filled, a confession of sin, and a yielding of oneself to the Holy Spirit's control. This simple process will result in the power of the Holy Spirit's working in our lives to give us ongoing victory over the world, the flesh, and the devil! Like tributaries flowing into the Amazon, it is God the Holy Spirit who fills us and takes control. It is God who can and will revive us to enjoy the Christian life to its fullest. Jesus said in John 10:10 *"…I am come that they might have life, and that they might have it more abundantly."*

Perhaps you have never received the life of which John 10:10 speaks. Maybe you have tried religion, works, self-improvement, or some man-made plan of salvation. None of these will give spiritual life. Ephesians 2:1 states, *"And you hath he quickened…."* This simply means "to be made alive." In John 14:6, Jesus said, *"…I am the way, the truth, and the life…."* You must see yourself as a sinner and recognize that your sin condemns you to separation from God in a place called Hell. Turn to Christ! Abandon all else. Totally trust in Jesus Christ as payment for your sins. Receive Him as Saviour.

Those who receive Christ have received life and are eternally secure in Him. Yet many who have this life are far from enjoying the fullness of life that Jesus gives. They have settled for hamburgers when they could enjoy steak!

Some men settle in for the long haul and determine not to be surrendered. They are not willing to be broken before the Lord. These men want to remain unchanged (a trickle), not willing to empty self of the weight and sin in their lives which hinder the tributaries of God's almighty power and presence from flowing through them. I cannot be of help to these men. I can only pray that God would get a hold of their lives and change their hearts and attitudes.

If you desire to be filled and controlled by the Holy Spirit and will allow the Lord to give a fresh reviving, here are five steps you can take which will allow you to experience continual revival.

Keep Yourself from the Accursed Thing (Sin)

In Joshua 6, Israel had just entered the Promised Land and faced the stronghold of Jericho. God gave Joshua a plan to defeat Jericho, and a great victory took place. Joshua warned all of the people not to take anything out of Jericho, "...*keep yourself from the accursed thing...*" (Joshua 6:18).

One man, Achan, disobeyed and his sin brought defeat in the next battle at Ai. When Achan's sin was discovered and he was confronted, his explanation was, "I saw, I coveted, and I took." Thirty-six men died as a result of his sin!

Your sin affects others. Even one seemingly small sin can rob us of victory and cause defeat. Hebrews 12:1 says to "...*lay aside every weight, and the sin that doth so easily beset us....*" The Christian man who truly wants to be a godly man must guard himself from the accursed thing.

Every man knows where his greatest struggles and temptations lie. First Corinthians 10:13 tells us, *"There hath no temptation taken you but such as is common to man: but God is faithful, who will not suffer you to be tempted above that ye are able; but will with the temptation also make a way to escape, that ye may be able to bear it."* By God's power, you can say no to sin (sin is a choice) and keep yourself from "the accursed thing."

When you do sin, confess it. *"If we confess our sins, He is faithful and just to forgive us our sins, and to cleanse us from all unrighteousness"* (1 John 1:9).

Keep Yourself from Idols

First John 5:21 states, *"Little children, keep yourselves from idols. Amen."* Many men think they have no idols in their lives—no carved or wooden images, no ceramic or metal statues. But anyone or anything that takes priority or preeminence over God is an idol (both a sin and a weight that slows us down).

Many idols can abound in our lives—computers, TV programs, sports, hobbies, recreational activities, and friends. Even a car or a pick-up truck could be an idol. Do you spend more time washing, working, and tinkering on that vehicle than you spend with the Lord? For many, money is an idol.

First Timothy 6:9–11 states, *"But they that will be rich fall into temptation and a snare, and into many foolish and hurtful lusts, which drown men in destruction and perdition. For the love of money is the root of all evil: which while some coveted after, they have erred from the faith, and pierced themselves through with many sorrows. But thou, O man of God, flee these things; and follow after righteousness, godliness, faith, love, patience, meekness."*

When we fail to put the Lord first, anything we put before Him is an idol. Proverbs 3:9 states, *"Honour the LORD with thy substance, and with the first fruits of all thine increase."* Idols occupy our time in such a way that they keep us from surrendering to the Lord and living our lives by His priorities.

What idol occupies your life? What takes the place of Christ having preeminence in your heart, robbing you of precious time in the Word and with the Lord? Even seemingly small idols need to be dealt with. Remember 1 John 5:21, *"Little children, keep yourselves from idols. Amen"*! As you become spiritually revived, determine to keep old idols from creeping back into your life.

Keep Yourself in the Love of God

Jude 21 states, *"Keep yourselves in the love of God...."* I thank God that His love for me is an unconditional love (always there), but I must keep my love and affections upon my Lord. This is a daily, moment-by-moment choice.

It was said of a very commendable church in Ephesus in Revelation 2:4, *"...I have somewhat against thee, because thou hast left thy first love."* Do you still have a fresh, powerful love for Christ like you did when you accepted Him as your Saviour? How easy it is to allow our love for the Lord to grow cold! Matthew 24:12 states, *"And because iniquity shall abound, the love of many shall wax cold."*

Colossians 3:1–2 states, *"If ye then be risen with Christ, seek those things which are above, where Christ sitteth on the right hand of God. Set your affection on things above, not on things on the earth."* Where are your affections? You love what you focus on! Keep yourself in love with the Lord through daily reading of God's Word, communion in prayer (fellowship with your Lord—talking to Him), and faithfulness to God's house (fellowship with other believers). Christ established the church and commanded us not to forsake the assembling of ourselves together (Hebrews 10:25).

These disciplines of the Word, prayer, and church attendance will make a great difference in keeping your love for the Lord revived and growing strong. Just as a husband and wife must daily work at feeding the fires of a growing love, thus it is with our relationship with God!

Keep His Words

John 14:23 says *"…If a man love me, he will keep my words."* God has wonderfully preserved His Word for us to read, to know, and then to obey. Second Peter 3:18 says, *"But grow in grace* (living), *and in the knowledge* (understanding) *of our Lord and Saviour Jesus Christ…."* Obedience to God's Word will keep your heart in a spirit of revival.

Rebellion and disobedience from children bring conflict and struggles in the home. Likewise, when we willfully disobey God's Word and rebel in our hearts, it brings turmoil and conflict in our lives—our walk with God becomes frustrating and broken.

In Acts 5:32 we read *"And we are his witnesses of these things; and so is also the Holy Ghost, whom God hath given to them that obey him."* Walking in obedience and keeping God's Word brings peace and revival to our souls. Disobedience quenches and grieves the Holy Spirit, rendering His power in our lives inoperative. Stay revived by keeping His Word!

Keep Your Heart

Proverbs 4:23 tells us, *"Keep thy heart with all diligence; for out of it are the issues of life."* This is the final key to experiencing continual revival in our lives. We must "keep"—guard and protect—our hearts from any wrong attitude or motive. So often we can find our hearts filled with anger, bitterness, and strife, and thus we quench or grieve the indwelling Holy Spirit. Be so very careful to protect your heart attitude! The challenge is found in 1 Thessalonians 5:19, *"Quench not the Spirit,"* and in Ephesians 4:30, *"And grieve not the holy Spirit of God…."*

The greatest battle we face with our attitudes is in our homes—with our wives and children. Colossians 3:19 says, *"Husbands, love your wives, and be not bitter against them."* Maintaining a right and loving spirit toward our wives is essential to keeping the fires of personal revival glowing in our hearts. In regard to our children, Colossians 3:21 tells us, *"Fathers, provoke not your children to anger, lest they be discouraged."* How is your attitude in your home? Are you guarding your heart toward these vital relationships?

Summary

We can enjoy continual revival in our lives as we live out these five keys to staying revived:

1. Keep Yourself from the Accursed Thing—besetting sins
2. Keep Yourself from Idols—anything that takes the place of God
3. Keep Yourself in the Love of God—through the Word of God, prayer, and church attendance
4. Keep His Word—walk in obedience
5. Keep Your Heart—right attitudes and motives

Don't be just a "trickle." Allow the tributaries of God's power and presence to fill you.

Action Steps

Here are three **Action Steps** to help keep you revived. (Initial and date when completed.)

1. List, in your mind or on a 3 x 5 card, the major besetting sins which seem to plague you the most.

   x_____   Date_____

2. Think of several steps to avoid and escape those besetting sins. (computer, TV, a place, a person, etc.)

   x_____   Date_____

3. On a 3 x 5 card, list the five steps to keep you revived. Review this card and refer to it regularly.

   x_____   Date_____

PART TWO

Nine Commitments of a Good Man

The first two chapters and actions will help you come into that closer and more vibrant relationship with God which results in having a genuine heart for God and experiencing real personal revival.

The following eight chapters are simply the commitments every good man should consider making to honor God and to enjoy the fullness of life and the wonderful relationships God has given him to enjoy. Continue to "grow in grace" or you will be "growing in disgrace." It is your choice to make by taking deliberate steps.

Daily Prayer

*Recognizing I can do nothing without Christ and I can
do all things through Him (Philippians 4:13), I will
ask God to supply all I need to do His will.*

CHAPTER THREE

Developing a Consistent Prayer Life

The subject of prayer has been the most written about, preached about, talked about subject, but the least practiced activity in the lives of most Christian men. We understand the importance of prayer, and no doubt the value of developing a consistent prayer life, yet we still fail to make prayer a vibrant part of our daily walk with God.

Prayer is the most powerful weapon the Lord has given to us, and yet it seems to be the one we use the very least. God does not intend for prayer to be used only in emergencies. He desires that we speak to Him on a daily, moment by moment basis. How would your relationship be with your wife if you only talked to her when you needed her help? Sadly, this is the way many Christian men treat God. They go to Him in prayer when things are going badly or if they need Him for something.

God wants to have a personal relationship with you which consists of *continual* communication. Communication is both giving and receiving information. As Christian men, we have become lazy. We go to church and hear *from* God all the time, but we don't find it important to talk *to* God.

One particular man in the Bible was a great example in this area of a consistent prayer life—Daniel. Daniel was faithful in his prayer life no matter what was going on around him or who was around to hear or see him. The Bible states that even after prayer was outlawed, he continued to pray as he had before, and God blessed him because of his faithfulness.

> *All the presidents of the kingdom, the governors, and the princes, the counselors, and the captains, have consulted together to establish a royal statute, and to make a firm decree, that whosoever shall ask a petition of any God or man for thirty days, save of thee, O king, he shall be cast into the den of lions. Wherefore king Darius signed the writing and the decree. Now when Daniel knew that the writing was signed, he went into his house; and his windows being open in his chamber toward Jerusalem, he kneeled upon his knees three times a day, and prayed, and gave thanks before his God, as he did aforetime.*—DANIEL 6:7, 9–10

The Bible tells us that he prayed three times daily! Perhaps you are thinking, "Well, I do too. Every time I eat a meal I give thanks for my food." Sometimes I wonder if God is honored when we quickly mumble a prayer for our food out of habit and not out of sincerity. Why do you give thanks for your food? These three times a day that Daniel set aside to pray were not just quick prayers. I believe these were the times when Daniel told God everything that was going on and then asked God for wisdom and discernment to make right choices. Daniel was one of the princes in Babylon, and he recognized that he needed God's help in making decisions. Instead of seeking worldly advice, he sought God's advice.

James tells us in James 1:5–6 *"If any of you lack wisdom, let him ask of God, that giveth to all men liberally, and upbraideth not; and it shall be given him. But let him ask in faith, nothing wavering. For he that wavereth is like a wave of the sea driven with the wind and tossed."* I don't really know what Daniel prayed about, but looking at what the Bible says about him gives me a good idea that he was not just praying for things he wanted or for the problems in his life. It is obvious to me that he was spending quality time with the One who ruled his life. If Christian men would place this kind of importance on prayer, we would have fewer problems in our homes and in our churches as a result.

A consistent prayer life does not happen overnight. It takes work. You don't just wake up one morning and decide, "I think I'll pray for an hour this morning." Some people may be able to do this, but most will not be able to keep it up for very long.

Paul said in 1 Corinthians 15:31, *"...I die daily."* Each day, we choose either to die to self or to live *for* ourselves. Paul was one of the greatest Christians who ever lived, yet he struggled daily. The only way Paul was able to live a victorious Christian life was by crucifying his flesh daily and seeking God's wisdom in every decision.

God created and controls everything, and He wants you to come to Him in prayer with even the smallest problems. He is interested in your little problems as well as your big ones! You might say you have surrendered your life to God, but if you are not consulting Him about even the little decisions, who is really in control?

Dr. John Goetsch often says, "Only two choices on the shelf, pleasing God or pleasing self." Which will you choose today? Your life will never be the same once you begin spending quality time in prayer with God each day.

Here are some recommendations that I hope will help you begin developing a *consistent* prayer life.

Plan Prayer Time

It has been said, "If you aim at nothing, you will hit it every time." Schedule a time for prayer. Jesus regularly arose early in the morning. He went to a solitary place to pray. Mark 1:35 reads, *"And in the morning, rising up a great while before day, he went out, and departed into a solitary place, and there prayed."*

Other men were wise in establishing scheduled times of prayer. Daniel prayed three times a day. General Havelock arose at four every morning and spent two hours in prayer. Martin Luther said, "I have so much to do that I cannot get on without three hours a day in prayer."

We seem to find time for everything except prayer, and that reveals how small a priority it truly is. Plan a regular time of prayer for yourself—in the prayer closet alone—and with your family (your wife and children). Make up a prayer list of specific needs you have, and list the names of people you desire to uphold in prayer.

If you live by a schedule, take time to schedule your prayer time throughout the day. If you do not live by a schedule, set up reminders, and make time to just stop and talk to God. You do not need to spend enormous amounts of time in prayer. It is not the quantity of time that changes you, but the quality of time with God. God would be pleased if you gave Him fifteen minutes a day, as long as it was quality time with Him.

Prepare for Prayer Time

When you start up an older car on a chilly morning, it usually sputters and coughs until it is warmed up. Likewise, in our prayer time, we need to get "warmed up"—ready to pray. Robert Murray McCheyne said, "A great part of my time is spent in getting my heart ready for prayer."

One way you could prepare for prayer is by reading the Psalms or other portions of Scripture. Read until you find yourself in the right frame of mind. A book that has had a great influence upon me regarding prayer is *Intercessor* by Norman Grubb. This book helped me realize the great necessity to prepare my heart for a season of prayer. It challenges the Christian to wait on the Lord and meditate upon the Lord.

Prevail in Prayer Time

Real prayer is hard work! It involves labor and travail. To get a hold of God we must pray in faith, believing. We need to take God at His word in prayer, claiming His promises.

In D.L. Moody's book *Prevailing Prayer*, he gives these basic elements of prayer:

Adoration
Confession
Restitution
Thanksgiving
Forgiveness
Unity
Faith
Petition
Submission

E. M. Bounds said, "Prayer can do anything that God can do." In James 5:16–17, we read "…*The effectual fervent prayer of a righteous man availeth much. Elias was a man subject to like passions as we are, and he prayed earnestly that it might not rain: and it rained not on the earth by the space of three years and six months.*"

J. Sidlow Baxter stained his study walls with his tears and his praying breath, and hundreds were swept into the Kingdom. David Brainerd ministered alone among the American Indians. His whole life was a life of prevailing prayer—he prayed day and night, before and after preaching, riding on his horse, on a bed of straw—hour by hour, day by day, and week by week.

Pray Effectively

Let me conclude with some thoughts about having an effective prayer life. There is not a man walking with God who is not interested in having an effective prayer life. Remember James 5:16. *"... The effectual fervent prayer of a righteous man availeth much."* There are always important issues that demand our time and attention, so it is vital that we learn how to pray effectively.

To this end, one important means to developing an effective prayer life would be to look at and study the lives and the prayers of those who have seen miraculous answers to prayer. Such an example is an Old Testament king named Hezekiah. Notice that King Hezekiah had a big problem:

> *Then Rabshakeh stood and cried with a loud voice in the Jews' language, and spake, saying, Hear the word of the great king, the king of Assyria: Thus saith the king, Let not Hezekiah deceive you: for he shall not be able to deliver you out of his hand: Neither let Hezekiah make you trust in the LORD, saying, The LORD will surely deliver us, and this city shall not be delivered into the hand of the king of Assyria. Hearken not to Hezekiah: for thus saith the king of Assyria, Make an agreement with me by a present, and come out to me, and then eat ye every man of his own vine, and every one of his fig tree, and drink ye every one the waters of his own cistern:—2 KINGS 18:28–31*

Although Hezekiah had trusted in the Lord and had done that which was right, he was still faced with the Assyrians knocking at his door. Sennacherib had sent three of his lieutenants to Jerusalem with a great host of Assyrian soldiers. The spokesman for this terrible trio taunted the Israelites, ridiculing their faith in the Lord.

When Hezekiah heard that the Assyrians were outside the walls, he rent his clothes, covered himself with sackcloth and ashes, and went to the house of the Lord. Isaiah, the prophet, encouraged him in 2 Kings 19:6–7, *"And Isaiah said unto them, Thus shall ye say to your master, Thus saith the* LORD, *Be not afraid of the words which thou hast heard, with which the servants of the king of Assyria have blasphemed me. Behold, I will send a blast upon him, and he shall hear a rumour, and shall return to his own land; and I will cause him to fall by the sword in his own land."* Then Hezekiah received a letter from the king of Assyria. What Hezekiah did next was characteristic of a person of faith. He prayed.

Notice this element of effectual, righteous prayer. When Hezekiah received a threatening letter from the king of Assyria, he immediately spread the letter before the Lord. There was no thought of calling in a committee! His first thought was to take this matter to the Lord and cast it upon Him.

When you face a difficult and almost impossible situation, upon what or whom do you call? Do you call a friend or relative? Do you take Valium and go to bed? Do you get angry and retaliate? The first thing you *should* do is go to God in prayer. Why is it that so often prayer is the last resort rather than the first?

Second Kings 19:15–16 reads, *"And Hezekiah prayed before the* LORD, *and said, O* LORD *God of Israel, which dwellest between the cherubims, thou art the God, even thou alone, of all the kingdoms of the earth; thou hast made heaven and earth.* LORD, *bow down thine ear, and hear: open,* LORD, *thine eyes, and see: and hear the words of Sennacherib, which hath sent him to reproach the living God."* Hezekiah immediately focused upon the majesty, power, and might of his God. We need to remind ourselves of and acknowledge before God, His attributes and sovereignty. Verse 16 states, *"...bow down thine ear and hear."* This passage acknowledges God as sovereign, but also recognizes Him as a friend.

In the New Testament, the expression "Abba Father" is used to demonstrate the type of close and intimate fellowship we should have with God. It is a very tender and endearing expression referring to God as "tender papa." We have a good, gracious, and generous Heavenly Father.

Hezekiah did not demand anything of his God as to what should be done; he was simply reminding himself of what God had already promised and how desperately he needed God. God already knows our situations, and He knows we need His divine intervention. He is simply waiting for us to come to Him in prayer—to acknowledge our need of Him and to invite His hand to work in our circumstances and in our hearts.

In 2 Kings 19:19 we read, *"Now therefore, O LORD our God, I beseech thee, save thou us out of his hand…."* The time had come to get down to business. Hezekiah pointedly made his request known to God. He did not mince words but directly said, *"Save thou us out of his hand…."* He did not try to tell God how to solve the problem, he just asked God for deliverance and then committed his problem to the Lord.

Second Kings 19:19 continues, *"…that all the kingdoms of the earth may know that thou art the LORD God, even thou only."* It is important that everything we request is for God's praise and glory—not for our benefit alone. Anything that happens to God's people is a direct reflection of God's purposes. Our motivation to pray should be that the world would see the grace and glory of God as He delivers us from desperate situations.

In 2 Kings 19:35–36 we read, *"And it came to pass that night, that the angel of the LORD went out, and smote in the camp of the Assyrians an hundred fourscore and five thousand: and when they arose early in the morning, behold, they were all dead corpses. So Sennacherib king of Assyria departed, and went and returned, and dwelt at Nineveh."*

Early the next morning Hezekiah and the Jews found their enemies, the Assyrians, routed, and 185,000 dead Assyrian soldiers lay on the ground.

God heard Hezekiah's prayer and delivered him. "...*the effectual fervent prayer of a righteous man availeth much.*" You can rest assured that your God is ready and waiting to hear your prayer and to intervene in your life! Hezekiah's God is your God and He hasn't changed!

As a growing, godly man, will you make this first commitment? Will you follow the example of so many godly men before you? Will you follow the example of Hezekiah? Commit to seeking God and meeting Him in a daily, vibrant time of personal prayer—seeking His face and casting yourself in full dependence upon Him. A godly man makes daily prayer a life commitment, and this first commitment will give way to an amazing work of God in every area of life.

Summary

If we are going to be godly men, we must engage ourselves in developing consistent prayer lives. Many other tasks, activities, and opportunities can and will rob us of the activity of prayer, but we must make the decision to keep prayer a priority in our daily walk.

1. Plan Prayer Time
2. Prepare for Prayer Time
3. Prevail in Prayer Time
4. Pray Effectively

Action Steps

Here are three **Action Steps** you can take to make prayer a priority. (Initial and date when completed.)

1. Begin a simple prayer list on a 3 x 5 card, putting down key people and matters you are praying about.

   x_____ Date_____

2. Schedule a minimum of two prayer times each day at specific times, praying a minimum of five minutes.

   x_____ Date_____

3. Pray with someone, preferably your wife, regarding specific areas of need and blessings.

   x_____ Date_____

Daily Control of the Holy Spirit in My Life

Realizing I am, by nature, a selfish person wanting to be served rather than to serve, I will surrender myself daily to the Holy Spirit's control to be the servant-leader God wants me to be (Ephesians 5:18–20).

CHAPTER FOUR

Living in the Control
of the Holy Spirit

One of the greatest benefits and blessings for every Christian man is that at the moment of salvation, the Holy Spirit came to take up residence in that man's life. First Corinthians 6:19–20 reads, *"What? know ye not that your body is the temple of the Holy Ghost which is in you, which ye have of God, and ye are not your own? For ye are bought with a price: therefore glorify God in your body, and in your spirit, which are God's."*

At salvation, not only did the Holy Spirit indwell you, but you were spiritually baptized into Christ. First Corinthians 12:13 says, *"For by one Spirit are we all baptized into one body, whether we be Jews or Gentiles, whether we be bond or free; and have been all made to drink into one Spirit."* You are in Him and He (Christ) is in you through the person of the Holy Spirit. *"At that day ye shall know that I am in my Father, and ye in me, and I in you"* (John 14:20).

You are also sealed by the blessed Holy Spirit until the day of redemption. *"And grieve not the holy Spirit of God, whereby ye are sealed unto the day of redemption"* (Ephesians 4:30). You have One living within you who is always there to lead and guide. *"Howbeit when he, the Spirit of truth, is come, he will guide you into all truth: for he shall not speak of himself; but whatsoever he shall hear, that shall he speak: and he will shew you things to come"* (John 16:13).

Ephesians 5:18 states a commandment to be fully controlled and filled by the Holy Spirit. Though the Holy Spirit indwelled you at the moment of salvation, the question of control is a moment-by-moment consideration. You always have Him, but does He have you? Does the Holy Spirit of God control your thoughts, your attitudes, your desires, and your daily actions? He is ready to take the reins of your life if you will yield to Him.

The Problem of Control

Even after salvation, we still wrestle with the flesh, and we find a measure of struggle exists on a daily basis because the Holy Spirit and our flesh are at odds with one another. Galatians 5:17 says, *"For the flesh lusteth against the Spirit, and the Spirit against the flesh: and these are contrary the one to the other: so that ye cannot do the things that ye would."*

When we allow our flesh to control our lives, we express and experience the works of the flesh—*"Now the works of the flesh are manifest, which are these; Adultery, fornication, uncleanness, lasciviousness, Idolatry, witchcraft, hatred, variance, emulations, wrath, strife, seditions, heresies, Envyings, murders, drunkenness, revellings, and such like"* (Galatians 5:19–21). When we walk in the Spirit we will demonstrate the fruit of the Spirit—*"But the fruit of the Spirit is love, joy, peace, longsuffering, gentleness, goodness, faith, Meekness, temperance: against such there is no law"* (Galatians 5:22–23).

My good friend, Dr. Tom Wallace, has often asked the question, "Are you right now filled with the Spirit?" The great need and a genuine mark of a godly man is that he lives under the moment by moment control of the Holy Spirit every day.

When any sin in word, thought, or deed enters our lives, we quench the Holy Spirit. *"Quench not the Spirit"* (1 Thessalonians 5:19); or we grieve the Holy Spirit, *"And grieve not the holy Spirit of God…"* (Ephesians 4:30). We render the Holy Spirit inoperative, and we bind Him, thus allowing fleshly appetites and self-will to prevail.

The Holy Spirit's baptism and indwelling occurs once at salvation; however, we can and must experience many *fillings* of the Spirit day by day. This fresh filling of the Spirit should happen whenever we quench or grieve the Spirit because of any sin that has entered our lives.

The Procedure for Control

Many years ago, in Bible college, a wonderful truth was conveyed to me by one of my instructors, Jim Huckleby. This simple and biblical formula helped me understand how quickly and simply I could enjoy the filling and control of the blessed Holy Spirit once again. Desire + Confess + Yield + Appropriate = Power. Let's break this down and understand the formula.

Desire. I must first have a desire to be right with God and to enjoy the filling of the Spirit. Mark 11:24 says, *"Therefore I say unto you, What things soever ye desire, when ye pray, believe that ye receive them, and ye shall have them."* Colossians 3:1 says, *"If ye then be risen with Christ, seek those things which are above, where Christ sitteth on the right hand of God."* Setting our desires and attention on truly wanting to glorify God and walking in the control of the Holy Spirit, is the first step to being filled with Him.

Confess. We must understand that our sinful actions or attitudes have quenched or grieved the Holy Spirit, and sin must be dealt with. *"If we confess our sins, he is faithful and just to forgive us our sins, and to cleanse us from all unrighteousness"* (1 John 1:9).

Thank God for this wonderful means to keep the heart clean and the conscience clear with the Saviour. Acknowledge and confess your sin, agreeing with God about your wicked and fleshly actions and attitudes. Then accept by faith that you are clean and rest in the understanding that He has fully cleansed and forgiven you.

Yield. This simple third step is a matter of surrender—acknowledging to the Lord your desire to be under the filling and control of the Spirit. *"Neither yield ye your members as instruments of unrighteousness unto sin: but yield yourselves unto God, as those that are alive from the dead, and your members as instruments of righteousness unto God"* (Romans 6:13). It involves saying something as simple as this: "Lord Jesus, right now I yield the control of my life to you. I surrender my will, my thoughts, my whole self to the filling and guidance of your Holy Spirit. Please take control and live through me this moment!" This is something that you will find needs to be done frequently throughout the day.

Appropriate. By faith, understand, believe, and know that you are now once again under the Holy Spirit's control. *"And whatsoever we ask, we receive of him, because we keep his commandments, and do those things that are pleasing in his sight"* (1 John 3:22). We are told in 2 Corinthians 5:7, *"For we walk by faith, not by sight."* Thank the Lord for this fresh filling of the Holy Spirit and believe that He is once again controlling your life.

Power. The result of allowing the Holy Spirit to control your life is having the subsequent power in your life that only He can provide. You can be sure that your thoughts, your emotions, your actions, and your lifestyle will be different from what they would have been. You will have wisdom, discernment, and insight that you would not have had. Your relationships and your whole life will benefit from this wonderful new power!

This simple formula has helped me scores of times over the years. It is vital for every Christian man to develop a consistently Spirit-filled life if he is going to be the right kind of godly man, husband, and father. Walking in the Spirit's control provides us power for victory, prevents us from sinning, equips us for service, and gives us guidance through life's journey.

The Potential for Ministry

Every man who desires to honor his Master should use the spiritual gifts that he was given at the moment of salvation, through faithful service in his local church. Paul states in 1 Corinthians 12:1, *"Now concerning spiritual gifts, brethren, I would not have you ignorant."* In Romans 12:3–8, 1 Corinthians 12:1–31, and Ephesians 4:11–13, there are eighteen different spiritual gifts listed. Of these, there are five that I would list as temporary, or "sign gifts", which most Bible students would agree ceased at the completion of the canon of Scriptures.

I once heard of a man who bought a used table saw. He was very excited and went into the garage to plug it in, but immediately the saw sounded "tired," and when a piece of wood was put in, it bogged down and failed to cut adequately. He concluded that perhaps the motor was worn out and needed to be replaced. It was only then that he noticed the electrical information on the side instructed to use 220 volts. He had been trying to operate on 110 volts.

Most Christian men are operating on 110 volts in serving God—they are operating way under power. Why? Usually because they do not understand what their spiritual giftedness is, and they are not using their gifts in the power of the Spirit to serve God and His people.

Spiritual gifts are the channel through which the Holy Spirit can minister in the local church. He has gifted you and enabled you to serve Him in a unique way, and it is through your spiritual gifts that the Holy Spirit will fully reveal Himself in a functional way in your life.

Jesus Christ left us with the Great Commission in Matthew 28:19–20, *"Go ye therefore, and teach all nations, baptizing them in the name of the Father, and of the Son, and of the Holy Ghost: Teaching them to observe all things whatsoever I have commanded you: and, lo, I am with you alway, even unto the end of the world. Amen."* We are to reach and teach others!

Jesus Christ also gave us the power and ability to accomplish great things through the *gifts* of the Holy Spirit (Luke 11:13 and Ephesians 4:7–8). Remember, Paul said in 1 Corinthians 12:1, *"Now concerning spiritual gifts, brethren, I would not have you ignorant"* (lacking in knowledge).

Let's see several spiritual gifts listed in Scripture. Notice in 1 Corinthians 12:8–10, there are four gifts listed:

> *For to one is given by the Spirit the word of wisdom; to another the word of knowledge by the same Spirit; To another faith by the same Spirit; to another the gifts of healing by the same Spirit; To another the working of miracles; to another prophecy; to another discerning of spirits; to another divers kinds of tongues; to another the interpretation of tongues:*

1. Wisdom (v. 8). This is the supernatural capacity to apply and powerfully impart spiritual knowledge. It is a gift that is greatly needed in churches today. Many of God's people are lacking in wisdom. Wrong and tragic decisions are being made that could literally bring ruin and disaster to individuals and families.

James 1:5 reads, *"If any of you lack wisdom, let him ask of God, that giveth to all men liberally, and upbraideth not, and it shall be given him."* Many believers have this gift but never develop it. Every believer needs to seek for God's wisdom. But God also gives the gift of wisdom to people within a local church to help and to give direction. Proverbs tells us that there is safety in a multitude of counselors (Proverbs 24:6).

When was the last time you were faced with an important decision and you sought counsel from the pastor/shepherd, or another godly Christian—one who has been walking with the Lord many years? You will ultimately have to make the decision, but *seek wisdom*—first from God and then from godly people in your local church.

2. Knowledge (v. 8). This is the Spirit-given capacity to learn and comprehend God's revealed truth. This gift, like the gift of prophesy, seems to have faded away (1 Corinthians 13:8) when the Bible was completed, particularly regarding direct or oral revelation from God. However, as this gift could be applied to God-written revelation, some could have the gift of knowledge in understanding and communicating Bible truth.

Second Timothy 2:15 says, *"Study to shew thyself approved...."* We need to study and know the Word of God. Praise God for those who have made the study of God's Word a major activity in their lives. Wisdom, knowledge, faith, and discernment all increase and are strengthened by studying the Bible.

3. Faith (v. 9). This is the Spirit-given capacity to believe and expect great things from God. Hebrews 11:6 says, *"But without faith it is impossible to please him...."* There is saving faith, and there is maturing faith, *"...according as God hath dealt to every man the measure of faith"* (Romans 12:3). We need to grow in our faith. We should pray, "Lord, help thou our unbelief...." One great example of a man with the gift of faith was George Mueller, a man who literally prayed for and saw God provide millions of dollars to establish orphanages for the homeless children in England.

There are those who believe God and expect great and miraculous things from God. Faith is linked to prayer, and many times the gift of faith is given to great people of prayer.

4. Discernment (v. 10). Discernment is the supernatural capacity to distinguish between truth and error, between the Holy Spirit, man's spirit, and demonic spirits. This gift is greatly lacking in Bible-believing circles today. There is so much error in doctrines preached, principles practiced, and activities performed. Many Christians and even pastors are deceived and misled by neo-evangelicalism, the cults, and the acceptance of compromise. First John 4:1 says, *"Beloved, believe not every spirit, but try the spirits whether they are of God: because many false prophets are gone out into the world."*

5. Serving. (Romans 12:7, 1 Corinthians 12:28, 1 Peter 4:9) Serving is the gift of ministering, helping, and hospitality. It is a gift used in the broadest sense. Every Christian can serve and use this gift for God's glory. There are many ways you can help and minister. You could be available to help set up or clean up for a fellowship time, help maintain the vehicles at church, or help with yard or building maintenance. Be a blessing to the church by offering your serving gifts to minister in any way possible!

6. Teaching. (Romans 12:7, 1 Corinthians 12:28) Teaching is a God-given ability to explain and apply the details of God's revelation—the Bible. Many times it is a single gift given to a person, and it is always a gift given to a man who is called to be a pastor or teacher. The gift of teaching can and should be developed through training, schooling, and experience. Many Christians have this gift and need to exercise it. This gift comes with a desire, interest, or ability to teach.

7. Pastor or Teacher. (Ephesians 4:11) The word *pastor* means "to shepherd;" therefore, this gift involves leading, teaching, providing, caring for, and protecting the God-given flock that has been committed to his care. There are four different words for the same office—pastor, elder, bishop, and presbyter. These refer to the same office but to different aspects of that calling. It is a God-given gift and calling. Some who were called are out of the ministry today and are very frustrated. Some have never surrendered to the calling of this gift.

8. Evangelism. (Ephesians 4:11) The meaning of this gift seems to be divided into two different ideas.

Evangelism is proclaiming a message—the good news of salvation. Every born again believer has been called and commissioned to give out the Gospel message, to be an ambassador or representative of Jesus Christ and a witness of the risen Saviour. Nowhere in Scripture is this task of spreading the Gospel given to a select group. All are included. There is no "gift" of soulwinning; however, some have a unique ability to lead scores of people to Christ.

An *evangelist* is a person who has the gift of evangelism and carries a message on an itinerant ministry (going to various places proclaiming the Gospel). The Apostle Paul had the gift of an evangelist (Acts 19). Philip was an evangelist (Acts 21:8). Paul told young Timothy in 2 Timothy 4:5, "...*do the work of an evangelist...*" —preach the Gospel, the Good News.

9. Prophesy. (Romans 12:6, 1 Corinthians 12:10; 14:1–40, Ephesians 4:11) This word is used both in a general and a limited sense.

Forthtelling generally means to preach or speak forth a message from God. Thus the preacher is a prophet—forthtelling God's truth. The one prophesying receives his message from God's Word and is guided by God as he delivers the message.

Foretelling is the content of a message from God which contains unrevealed events of the future unknown to man. God often supernaturally revealed the future. This gift was needed and evidenced until the Bible was complete. There are no future revelations outside of Scripture, so this aspect of prophesying had only a limited use for a time.

10. Exhortation. (Romans 12:8) This gift involves encouraging, comforting, and admonishing people. It is serving God by motivating people to action in a right direction.

Positive exhortation encourages or comforts. Many discouraged and defeated saints need to be uplifted, encouraged and challenged.

Negative exhortation admonishes. Many believers are wayward by ignorance or willful disobedience. They need to be admonished and motivated to get their lives back on the right path.

In exercising any of these spiritual gifts, especially exhortation, remember that it is essential to exercise them with *love*. God is pleased when we lovingly admonish and exhort each other to press on for Him.

11. Giving. (Romans 12:8) This is serving God by giving material resources generously and with great liberality. God commands every believer to give back to the Lord His tithe, ten percent of all he receives. If a believer doesn't at least give the tithe, he is disobeying and robbing God!

Those who have the gift of giving, love to give with great generosity with no thought of return. Some who have this gift have not learned to exercise it or are unable to because they are in bondage to their bills through debt. Yet, quite often a person with this gift has the unique ability in his heart to love generosity! Usually God has sovereignly provided for this person to give in a special way.

If God has given you this gift, you must develop it and use it for His glory. Invest to the best of your ability into the local church and into the cause of Christ that has been put before you. According to 2 Corinthians 8:7, God wants you to *"...abound in this grace also."*

12. Administration. (Romans 12:8) Administration is the ability to rule, or govern wisely; it is the ability to lead well. It can be demonstrated by organizing and leading various affairs in the local church. Obviously this gift is very helpful to the pastor, yet others within the local church also have this gift. As a church grows and expands, it becomes necessary for more and more people to help organize and lead various ministries. I praise the Lord for those who are so capable and willing to step up and take areas of responsibility—to exercise their spiritual gift of administration. An old cliché says, "delegate or stagnate." If you have this gift, are you willing to use it in the Lord's work? It is needed!

13. Mercy. (Romans 12:8) Mercy identifies and comforts those in distress. There are many heavy hearts within your reach— because of broken homes, sickness, death, or financial setbacks. These are the people who need your gift of mercy. Jesus had mercy and compassion which He demonstrated everywhere He went.

This has been just a quick overview of the spiritual gifts that the Holy Spirit desires to use within us. Will you ask God to show you what gifts He has given you, and then begin to develop these gifts and use them in your home, your local church, and all aspects of your life?

This second commitment—living under the control of the Holy Spirit—is so vital to being a godly man! Will you surrender your life to Him right now? Will you wake up every morning with a new prayer on your lips— "Lord, today I am yours. Please fill me and control me today!" As you do, the Holy Spirit will control you and empower you. He will develop and use the unique gifts He has placed within you to serve God and His people. The Spirit-filled life is a wonderful, serving, transforming kind of life. Once you taste it, you will never want to live any other way!

Summary

In this chapter we saw three aspects of living in the control of the Holy Spirit and several gifts the Holy Spirit can develop in our lives.

1. The Problem of Control
2. The Procedure for Control
3. The Potential for Ministry—Spiritual Gifts

Action Steps

Here are three **Action Steps** you can take to begin "walking in the Spirit." (Initial and date when completed.)

1. Memorize Ephesians 5:18 and Galatians 5:22–23.

   x_____   Date_____

2. Mentally go through the four simple steps for the filling of the Holy Spirit and memorize them.

   x_____   Date_____

3. Ask yourself, periodically throughout the day, "Am I walking in the Spirit or in the flesh?"

   x_____   Date_____

The Daily Study of God's Word

Realizing that the Word of God is my only authority for faith and practice, I am committed to read, study, and obey the Word of God that I might be able to properly understand its truths and live by its precepts (2 Timothy 2:15; 3:16–17).

CHAPTER FIVE

Studying God's Word Daily

After a severe bombing in the town of Surrey, England, during World War II, a woman was found standing in the middle of the street weeping uncontrollably. She cried out, "I've lost it all, I've lost everything—my husband, my children, my home, and all my earthly possessions—everything!" Then she came to some measure of composure and stated, "I was wrong. I did not lose everything, for I still have my Saviour who will care for me, and I still have His precious Word," as she clutched her Bible to her heart.

The most precious and valuable possession we have outside of our blessed Saviour is His wonderful Word. By God's divine plan and sovereign direction, He has not only given us His inspired Word, but He has preserved and protected it down through the corridors of time.

> *Knowing this first, that no prophecy of the scripture is of any private interpretation. For the prophecy came not in*

old time by the will of man: but holy men of God spake as they were moved by the Holy Ghost.—2 PETER 1:20–21

Study to shew thyself approved unto God, a workman that needeth not to be ashamed, rightly dividing the word of truth. But shun profane and vain babblings: for they will increase unto more ungodliness. And their word will eat as doth a canker: of whom is Hymenaeus and Philetus;—2 TIMOTHY 2:15–17

For verily I say unto you, Till heaven and earth pass, one jot or one tittle shall in no wise pass from the law, till all be fulfilled.—MATTHEW 5:18

Thy word is true from the beginning: and every one of thy righteous judgments endureth for ever. —PSALM 119:160

It has been Satan's ongoing plan, since the beginning of time, to destroy, discredit, and dilute God's Word. Satan began way back in the Garden of Eden when he conversed with Eve after she stated in Genesis 3:2–3, "*…We may eat of the fruit of the trees of the garden: But of the fruit of the tree which is in the midst of the garden, God hath said, Ye shall not eat of it, neither shall ye touch it, lest ye die.*" Satan immediately responded in Genesis 3:4–5, "*…Ye shall not surely die: For God doth know that in the day ye eat thereof, then your eyes shall be opened, and ye shall be as gods, knowing good and evil.*"

Make no mistake about it, at this very moment, Satan continues to do everything within his power to attack God's Word. He has flooded the "Christian market" with a host of Bible versions, translations, paraphrases, and the like. There are over two hundred new English versions, and a new one is being printed every six months!

Stay with your good, old King James Version of the Bible, and rest assured, you have in your hands God's divine and preserved

Word. For many good reasons beyond the scope of this book, you can believe it and trust it with complete confidence. This is God's Word for the English speaking people today. Numerous good books are available that deal with the textual issue. Talk with your pastor if you want more information and material on this subject.

The greatest tragedy today in the lives of many Christian men is the neglect of God's Holy Word. His Word is an absolute necessity if we will be godly men—all that God wants us to be as Christian men, as husbands, and as fathers. Just as food provides strength and nutrients to your physical body for physical health, so the Word of God provides nourishment to your soul for spiritual health. The neglect of God's Word produces a weak, anemic, and carnal Christian man.

Think for a moment about the study of God's Word. The Bible says in John 14:15, "*If ye love me, keep my commandments.*" Our natural reaction to that is to say, "There's no way anyone could do that." Although we cannot keep all His commandments all the time, we can strive to do our best at keeping them.

The only way you can even come close to keeping His commandments is by first knowing them. I am not speaking of only knowing the Ten Commandments listed in Exodus 20, but also knowing all the other commandments listed throughout the Word of God. The way to find all of God's commandments is by reading His Word. You can't expect to learn of every commandment just by going to church every week. God expects you to do your part by getting into the Bible and studying for yourself. Gather some basic tools to aid you in your study of God's Word. Have a copy of the King James Version of the Bible, a good concordance, and a Bible dictionary. Many of these study helps are available in the form of computer software. These are the essential tools to begin studying the Word of God. See your pastor for his advice and suggestions for any other study items.

Next to prayer, one of the most difficult things for a Christian man to discipline himself to do faithfully is to read and study his Bible. We call ourselves Christian men, and we say we love the Lord Jesus, but do our actions say that we love Him? Do we schedule time to study His Word? This is one of the most important things a godly man will do on a daily basis.

From personal experience, when I don't read and study God's Word faithfully, it is much more difficult to walk in the power of the Holy Spirit. But when I spend time in my Bible on a daily basis, I find that God gives me just what I need to battle the temptations for that day and to live victoriously.

As we have already mentioned, the Bible says in 2 Timothy 2:15, *"Study to show thyself approved unto God...."* To give a wise response when someone asks a question about the Bible, we must study it regularly. First Peter 3:15 says, *"But sanctify the Lord God in your hearts: and be ready always to give an answer to every man that asketh you a reason of the hope that is in you with meekness and fear."* We should not be put to shame when someone starts to argue against what God says. We should know the answers and be able to give a proper response from the Word of God. If we are unable to give a response right away, we should study to find a proper answer. Being *"ready always to give an answer"* will only come through personal study. We can spend years in church services and Sunday school classes, but we will learn more of the Bible through personal study than in any other context.

How much do you enjoy reading God's Word? The psalmist said in Psalm 119:103, *"How sweet are thy words unto my taste! yea, sweeter than honey to my mouth!"* If God's Word was sweeter than honey to us, we would enjoy it every day. Honey, in Bible times, was probably the equivalent of today's sugar—it was used to sweeten everything. The word picture here is teaching us that we should enjoy God's Word so much that we have to have it every day—it should literally be sweet to our spiritual taste.

Some people say they just can't go without their coffee, Coke, chocolate, or some other "goody." But when you ask them about their Bible reading, you find that they can go days without it, and think they are doing just fine. If you cannot "live" without something earthly for one day, why would you choose to live without food for your *soul* for one day? As you read through Psalm 119 you can see how much this psalmist loved the Word of God. Almost every verse talks about God's Word. Reading God's Word every day should be one of your highest priorities.

Another reason to read God's Word daily is to cleanse our ways. This is stated in Psalm 119:9, "*Wherewithal shall a young man cleanse his way? by taking heed thereto according to thy word.*" We are not to merely read God's Word and then forget what it says. We are to pay attention, and live out what we have read. Apart from staying in the Word of God, there is no way to truly live out the Christian life—His words are essential to spiritual growth. Reading and meditating upon His Word is vital to growing and living lives that glorify God.

James 1:23–25 speaks about Christians who look into the Word of God and then walk away, forgetting what it taught them, "*For if any be a hearer of the word, and not a doer, he is like unto a man beholding his natural face in a glass: For he beholdeth himself, and goeth his way, and straightway forgetteth what manner of man he was. But whoso looketh into the perfect law of liberty, and continueth therein, he being not a forgetful hearer, but a doer of the work, this man shall be blessed in his deed.*" This passage teaches us to read God's Word and then to apply it to our daily lives—to practice and obey what He has said. Our lives will not change until we allow the Word of God to penetrate into our hearts—only then will change be real and supernatural from within.

In closing, let me suggest four simple thoughts to give direction regarding this matter of spending time in God's Word.

1. Admit it as the Word of God. Make sure you approach the Scriptures, as we have already mentioned, as God's inerrant, preserved Word. Make His Word the final authority for all of your life and family. *"Heaven and earth shall pass away, but my words shall not pass away"* (Matthew 24:35). Then ask God the Holy Spirit to lead and teach you as you open your Bible. The Holy Spirit will guide you into all truth (John 16:13). When you engage in the divine activity of reading God's Word, you can have great confidence that He is working in your life whether or not you sense it.

2. Commit it to your heart and life. Second Timothy 2:15 says to *"Study to shew thyself approved unto God, a workman that needeth not to be ashamed, rightly dividing the word of truth."* Not only are you to read the Bible daily through a planned method, but you are to study the Bible! The word *study* denotes the act of being diligent and applying yourself to know His Word. As mentioned, several good basic tools can help as you dig into the unsearchable riches of the Scriptures. Just as a diamond hunter will search and dig for rich treasure, so we must diligently apply ourselves.

My Uncle John Kliewer was a "rock hound" and was involved in lapidary work. He would go relentlessly looking and digging for specific kinds of rocks. He would then take them into his shop where he would labor and spend time cutting, chiseling, and polishing those precious stones. Like those precious stones, the Scriptures are full of great and precious truths that must be sought after and carefully studied out through Holy Spirit-led time and prayerful consideration.

I challenge you to commit to the careful study and application of God's Word. Do as the Bereans in Acts 17:11, *"These were more noble than those in Thessalonica, in that they received the word with all readiness of mind, and searched the scriptures daily, whether those things were so."* David said in Psalm 119:18, *"Open thou mine eyes, that I may behold wondrous things out of thy law."* God's Word will delight, inform, and change you as you read and study it.

3. Submit to it in simple obedience. Let God's Word do a work of transformation in your life as you practice the truths you read. Simply put, before you close God's Word, ask the Lord to show you some simple ways that you can practice what you have read. Perhaps you could set some small goal or make an action list for that day based upon God's truth. It is by this practical obedience to God's Word that you grow and are blessed. It is also by simple obedience that you are cleansed and are kept clean. Ephesians 5:26 says, *"That he might sanctify and cleanse it with the washing of water by the word."* Psalm 119:11 says, *"Thy word have I hid in mine heart, that I might not sin against thee."* A clean and a blessed life comes about by simple obedience in response to God's Word. Every time God's Word shows you some sin, wrong attitude, or act of rebellion, confess it, forsake it, and choose to obey the truth.

4. Transmit it to a lost world. The Word of God is pictured like a fire and a hammer in Jeremiah 23:29, *"Is not my word like as a fire? saith the LORD; and like a hammer that breaketh the rock in pieces?"* By the power of the Word, the hardest heart can be broken, as we faithfully present the Gospel. The greatest tool in soulwinning and the only tool that can save a soul is God's Word. Hebrews 4:12 tells us, *"For the word of God is quick, and powerful, and sharper than any twoedged sword, piercing even to the dividing asunder of soul and spirit, and of the joints and marrow, and is a discerner of the thoughts and intents of the heart."*

When we share God's Word in the power of His Spirit, God can use us to make a great impact. Be compassionately bold in presenting the Gospel as you give out the Scriptures. Romans 10:17 tells us, *"So then faith cometh by hearing, and hearing by the word of God."* We will cover more on this subject in another chapter.

Will you step up and make this third commitment? Will you make God's Word a daily priority in your life? Will you read it, study it, memorize it, obey it, and share it with others? The steps of a good man always lead to God's Word!

Summary

In this chapter we saw the importance of studying God's Word on a daily basis. As you make God's Word a priority in your life, you should:

1. Admit it as the Word of God—make it your authority.
2. Commit it to your heart and life—read it and study it.
3. Submit to it in simple obedience—make an action list.
4. Transmit it to a lost world—share it with others.

Action Steps

Here are three **Action Steps** you can take to develop your time in the Word. (Initial and date when completed.)

1. Read through Psalm 119 once a day for a week.

    x_____   Date_____

2. Take time with some tools to study the passage of John 15:1–14 regarding the vine and the branches.

    x_____   Date_____

3. Memorize Hebrews 4:12.

    x_____   Date_____

COMMITMENT 4

Regular Support of a Fundamental, Bible-believing Church

Realizing that the local church is God's instrument for reaching our world today and is God's pillar and ground of truth for our society, I will faithfully support my local church with my attendance, my tithes, and my offerings (1 Timothy 3:15, Hebrews 10:24–25).

CHAPTER SIX

Faithfully Supporting
My Local Church

S ome men view the Christian faith as a crutch—merely some sort of emotional or psychological support structure for weak-minded people. Nothing could be farther from the truth, and this way of thinking really ignores some very important facts. First of all, these very men usually have their own personal vices that truly are physical or emotional dependencies—such as alcohol, pornography, sports, or a few buddies at the tavern. Sadly, these dependencies give the immediate sensation of relief and the ability to cope with and to escape from life's pressures, but at the same time they are destructive. It's a deceptive sort of pseudo-support.

Second, this rationale misses the fact that God didn't create us as independent beings in any way! For instance, even as you read this book, you are dependent upon a fresh breath of oxygen every few seconds—and if you failed to receive one, reading would quickly become your last priority! Today you will also be dependent upon food, water, rest, and physical strength. In much the same way, God has created you and me to be interdependent beings—dependent upon God and upon other healthy relationships in life. Like fresh air to our lungs and fresh water to our thirst, God has a spiritual and relational support structure upon which every man should rely for spiritual health and growth.

God's gift to us and His plan for us is for every born again believer to be an integral part of a fundamental, Bible-believing, Gospel preaching, local New Testament church. That is the long way of saying, "the right kind of church!" Not just any church will do; it must be a church that is patterned after God's biblical description.

Just as you can exist for a while on junk food or with little sleep, even so a man can be saved and go to Heaven without being a part of a local church. Yet, just as a lack of nourishment and sleep would adversely affect your health and eventually destroy you, so will your spiritual life suffer if you don't plant yourself firmly in a local, Bible-believing body of believers. Until you become grounded in a strong church, you will severely limit what God would do in and through you, and living for Christ will be much more laborious and frustrating. In addition to this, without a church you will also limit what God would do in the lives of your family members!

God ordained and established three primary institutions for our benefit and blessing. The first is the *home*. The family is an essential and key part of our lives. Second, God established *human government* for our protection and well-being, for a safe and healthy environment for our homes. Finally, God established and ordained the *local New Testament church* for our growth, spiritual health, and usefulness in His divine program. Tragically, all three of these institutions, in many cases, have gone awry from God's plan and pattern. However, that does not preclude our support and involvement in these institutions.

I read a story told by the late Dr. M. R. DeHaan of a local church congregation that bought an old tavern they wanted to convert into a church building. Enthusiastically they removed the bar, put in some new lights, installed pews, put in new carpet, and refurbished the entire building.

The old tavern keeper, however, had left behind his old parrot that had lived in the tavern for years. The wise old bird was perched high above in the rafter. On the first Sunday morning the Pastor walked in and the parrot exclaimed, "New proprietor, new proprietor!" The robed choir took their place, and the old bird squawked, "New floor show, new floor show!" Then the parrot looked out at the congregation and said, "Same old crowd, same old crowd."

There certainly is some humor in that story, but tragically, many churches today would fit this tale. The local New Testament church is to be an assembly of born again, blood-washed, and scripturally baptized believers. These members are to be new creatures in Christ Jesus. Second Corinthians 5:17 says, *"Therefore if any man be in Christ, he is a new creature: old things are passed away; behold, all things are become new."*

We are to be saved, separated unto God, and faithfully serving our Lord in His local church, as we discussed in chapter five— exercising our spiritual gifts by standing behind our pastor, the leadership, and faithfully supporting the work of Christ with our tithes and offerings.

As we focus on the local church in this chapter, we will develop a simple acrostic for the word "church" to help us better understand the purpose of the local church. The local church and the worship of the Lord on Sunday has lost much ground over the years. Our great grandfathers called it the Holy Sabbath, and our grandfathers called it the Sabbath Day. Then our fathers called it Sunday, the Lord's Day, and today we call it the weekend. May God help us to order our steps as godly men in a way that reverences His day and loves His church! Your life and family will never be the same if you will allow God to bless and grow you within a local body of Christians. Let's notice the following truths about the kind of local church you should attend.

Christ—the Head

Matthew 16:18 says, *"...upon this rock I will build my church...."* Ephesians 1:22–23 says, *"And hath put all things under his feet, and gave him to be the head over all things to the church, Which is his body, the fullness of him that filleth all in all."* And 1 Timothy 3:15 reads, *"But if I tarry long, that thou mayest know how thou oughtest to behave thyself in the house of God, which is the church of the living God, the pillar and ground of the truth."*

If someone were to walk up to a friend of yours and cut off his head, he would soon be dead! Likewise, any church where Christ is not the head, is a dead organism (organization). Revelation 3:20 says, *"Behold, I stand at the door, and knock...."* Many churches across America are dead because they have not allowed Christ to be the head of the church. A living church has Christ as its head!

Holy Spirit—the Power

A great quality of the church in the book of Acts was that it continually demonstrated unique *power.*

> *And when they had prayed, the place was shaken where they were assembled together; and they were all filled with the Holy Ghost, and they spake the word of God with boldness. And the multitude of them that believed were of one heart and of one soul: neither said any of them that ought of the things which he possessed was his own; but they had all things common. And with great power gave the apostles witness of the resurrection of the Lord Jesus: and great grace was upon them all.*—Acts 4:31–33

This was a great band of believers, because of the indwelling, control, and power of the Holy Spirit upon the church. In these three verses this church is described as being filled, bold, unified, having great power and great grace. The dynamic of the New Testament church was and still is the overwhelming, transforming power of the Holy Spirit. Ephesians 5:18 says, *"And be not drunk with wine, wherein is excess; but be filled with the Spirit."* Acts 4:14 states that the religious leaders marveled and noted that they (the apostles) had been with Jesus. These ignorant, unlearned men were accused of turning the world upside down!

One of the greatest untapped resources for the local church is the readily available dynamic power of the Holy Spirit! I remember standing by and watching the Niagara Falls several years ago and sensing the awesome power being harnessed by huge generators as the water surged over the precipice.

Today we have at our disposal an even greater power in the person of the Holy Spirit. Yet we feebly stumble along through life, powerless, defeated, and discouraged because we are not yielding to the power of the Holy Spirit. Acts 1:8 reads, *"But ye shall receive power, after that the Holy Ghost is come upon you...."* Can you imagine the dimension and dynamic of power available to you and to your church? We dare not waste His power!

Unsaved—the Mission

From the very beginning of the church and all through the book of Acts the mission of the church is to reach the unsaved world with the Gospel of Christ. Jesus gave the marching orders in Acts 1:8, *"But ye shall receive power, after that the Holy Ghost is come upon you: and ye shall be witnesses unto me both in Jerusalem, and in all Judaea, and in Samaria, and unto the uttermost part of the earth."*

Paul said, *"But we preach Christ crucified..."* (1 Corinthians 1:23). In the first century church, Christians didn't merely meet in some secluded room to seek for a "deeper life." Neither did they gather with a large crowd for a rock concert and a late night talk show environment. Tragically, today, most churches have lost their mission. Many churches have become nothing more than social gatherings designed to entertain and please men.

It is estimated that ninety-eight percent of all Christians will never lead a soul to Christ. The great mission of evangelization and personal soulwinning is non-existent in most Christians' lives. In spite of this, the heartbeat of the living God remains to see the Gospel proclaimed all over planet Earth through the work of His local church—and He desires for you to be a part of that local church and that global work.

The story is told of a young man who, four years after the sinking of the *Titanic*, stood up in a church meeting to give this testimony: "I am a survivor of the *Titanic*. When I was drifting alone on a spar that awful night, the tide brought Mr. John Harper, of Glasgow, also on a piece of wreck near me. 'Man,' he said, 'are you saved?' 'No,' I said. 'I am not.' He replied, 'Believe on the Lord Jesus Christ and thou shalt be saved.' The waves bore him away; but, strange to say brought him back a little later, and he said, 'Are you saved now?' 'No,' I said, 'I cannot honestly say that I am.' He said again, 'Believe on the Lord Jesus Christ, and thou shalt be saved,' and shortly after, he went down; and there, alone in the night, and with two miles of water under me, I believed. I am John Harper's last convert."

In the book of Acts we see the description of a dynamic testimony of great evangelism and soulwinning. The church multiplied greatly because the church had a mission to reach the unsaved. Everywhere they went, they talked to those around them about Christ. Every believer is a missionary, and every unbeliever is a mission field!

Revelation—the Authority

Everything we believe and practice must be supported by the Word of God, our final authority. In Acts 2, as Peter stood up to preach he quoted from Psalm 16:8–11, and as a result three thousand people were saved. The Apostle Paul told Timothy in 2 Timothy 4:2, *"Preach the word; be instant in season...."* First Timothy 3:15 says, *"...that thou mayest know how to behave thyself in the house of God, which is the church of the living God, the pillar and ground of the truth."*

Many so called "churches" today have multiple forms of authority—from traditions, to church leaders, to other various books and religious writings. The only authority for a local church should be the Word of God. Be sure you become a part of a church that bases all of its beliefs and practices purely upon the clear teaching of the Bible.

Thank God for His precious Word which He has given to us and preserved for our edification. The centerpiece of our pulpits is to be Bible preaching and the centerpiece of local church life should be learning and living out the Word.

Christians—the Body

The body is the called out assembly of the saved (Ephesians 1:22–23). Acts 2:42 and 47 describes what happened in the lives of those who were saved, *"And they continued stedfastly in the apostles' doctrine, and fellowship, and in breaking of bread, and in prayers. Praising God, and having favour with all the people. And the Lord added to the church daily such as should be saved."*

The church is a family—a body. We are many members, but we are one body where encouragement, unity, service, and fellowship should be the norm!

> *But speaking the truth in love, may grow up into him in all things, which is the head, even Christ: From whom the whole body fitly joined together and compacted by that which every joint supplieth, according to the effectual working in the measure of every part,*

maketh increase of the body unto the edifying of itself in love.—Ephesians 4:15–16

Heaven—the Hope

Philippians 3:20 says, "*For our conversation is in heaven; from whence also we look for the Saviour, the Lord Jesus Christ.*" Our destination is Heaven! We are a heavenly people and our churches should reflect a close-knit spirit of looking for that "blessed hope!"

Our hearts should be to strive together for the faith—to encourage, uplift, and press on together. We should strive to resolve problems and press upward for Christ together. That Christian you tend to fight and bicker with may be assigned to sit with you at the Marriage Supper!

Read about the marvelous place God is preparing for us in Revelation 21 and 22. First Corinthians 2:9 says, "*...Eye hath not seen, nor ear heard, neither have entered into the heart of man, the things which God hath prepared for them that love him.*" The next stop for the church is Heaven. Jesus is coming again!

I can truly testify that every good thing that has happened in my life took place in relation to the local church. Right after my birth, and even before, I was in church! My parents had my preacher dedicate me to the Lord and to the ministry at an early age. I got saved and was baptized in my local church and faithfully attended every service—Sunday morning, Sunday evening, and Wednesday night. When there were special meetings, my family attended. When I left home for Bible college, I met my dear wife at a Sunday church service as a freshman. I was married in church and called to preach in church. I raised my five children in church. Now so many years later—through trials and blessings alike, they are all faithfully living for the Lord and raising their own families in church!

I cannot emphasize enough the value and the importance of your faithfulness to your local church. If you will allow the Lord to order your steps—if you will become a godly man—it will involve growing and ministering faithfully in a local church. This fourth commitment is essential—it is God's plan for building your life, your family, and your future. Will you make this commitment? Will you join the long line of godly men through the centuries who have fully embraced God's plan? Find a Bible-believing church and plant yourself and your family there. Make a covenant with God that as long as He gives you breath, you will have a church and a pastor—you will have a place where you strive together with a family of believers for the faith of Christ.

Summary

In this chapter we saw the importance of the local church through this acrostic:

C   Christ—the Head

H   Holy Spirit—the Power

U   Unsaved—the Mission

R   Revelation—the Authority

C   Christians—the Body

H   Heaven—the Hope

Action Steps

Here are three **Action Steps** you can take to support your local church. (Initial and date when completed.)

1. Write a note of appreciation to your pastor, thanking him for his life and ministry.

    x_____   Date_____

2. Take a handful of your church brochures or tracts, and pass them out this week.

    x_____   Date_____

3. Look for some other opportunity to get involved in serving. Make sure you check with your pastor first.

    x_____   Date_____

Faithfulness to My God-given Wife

Realizing that my first obligation, as a husband, is to love my wife and to minister to her, I understand that I cannot be a faithful minister in any other area until first, I am properly loving my wife the way Christ loved the church (Ephesians 5:25). Therefore, I will develop a servant's heart in my home towards my wife, determining to show her the love of Christ no matter what her response is to me.

CHAPTER SEVEN

Strengthening My Relationship with My Wife

Years ago someone pointed out to me a wonderful verse in Proverbs 18:22, *"Whoso findeth a wife findeth a good thing, and obtaineth favor of the LORD."* I have found this verse to be absolutely true. For the joy and fulfillment of a man's life, a wife is needed to make him complete. This is true in the lives of most men; God created us this way. When God created Adam, He said in Genesis 2:18, *"...It is not good that the man should be alone: I will make him an help meet for him."* Woman is man's completer, and for the man who desires to be a godly man, no greater investment can be made than to care for and minister to his wife. Outside of the Lord Himself, your wife is the one whom God will use to make you all that you can be for God's glory.

Today, so many marriages and homes are in turmoil—even in Christian circles amongst people who claim to know and understand God's plan for marriage. The truth about this turmoil is that we as men are responsible for it! God says that the husband is to be the head of the wife and head of the home. I am not trying to shame you or guilt you if your family is experiencing turmoil—but simply hoping that you will step up as a leader and take responsibility for the spiritual condition of your home. The first step to leading your family in the right direction is taking responsibility for the fact that it is headed in the wrong direction. Notice God's instructions:

> *For the husband is the head of the wife, even as Christ is the head of the church: and he is the saviour of the body. Therefore as the church is subject unto Christ, so let the wives be to their own husbands in every thing. Husbands, love your wives, even as Christ also loved the church, and gave himself for it; That he might sanctify and cleanse it with the washing of water by the word, That he might present it to himself a glorious church, not having spot, or wrinkle, or any such thing; but that it should be holy and without blemish. So ought men to love their wives as their own bodies. He that loveth his wife loveth himself. For no man ever yet hated his own flesh; but nourisheth and cherisheth it, even as the Lord the church:*—EPHESIANS 5:23–29

These are sobering words of instruction and admonition for every husband. We are to sacrificially give ourselves to love and care for our wives. This is a choice, a decision to give of ourselves without any expectation of any favor or recognition in return. This is selfless, sacrificial love—like Christ loved the church. We are also told to "nourish" our wives in verse 29 which implies caring for them and supplying for them by being providers and loving leaders as the Lord nourishes us with His Word and by His grace. We are to "cherish" our wives—to nurture with tender love, protecting outwardly and providing soothing, comfortable rest inwardly. This is more than merely providing a home and grocery money—it involves meeting the physical as well as the deep, heartfelt emotional needs of our wives.

Being a biblically good husband seems to be a tall order! However, we already covered being filled with the Holy Spirit in a previous chapter, and by God's divine enablement we can become godly husbands day by day. Notice that the command to be filled with the Spirit is given just a couple verses before we are instructed on how to treat our wives! Men, it takes the grace of God and the power of the Holy Spirit to be the right kind of husband, and it takes time to grow and consistent training to become the right kind of husband.

I heard the story of the little four year old girl, Susie, who with wide-eyed excitement related to her mother how Prince Charming had arrived on his beautiful white horse and kissed Snow White back to life. "And do you know what happened then?" Susie asked. "Yes," said her mother, "They lived happily ever after." "No," responded little Susie, "They got married!"

In child-like innocence that little nursery school girl spoke the in-depth truth. Getting married and living happily ever after are not necessarily synonymous. Many marriages are struggling today, and the pattern quite often, even with Christian couples, is that divorce is the end result, bringing heartache, pain, dislocated children, financial hardship, and a lifetime of regret.

What are some things that help keep a lovelife glowing and growing? What keeps a relationship from growing sour and keeps freshness in that relationship? Allow me to give you seven keys to add mileage to your marriage, make the trip more enjoyable, and possibly save your marriage from wreckage.

In Colossians 3:12–14 Paul lists some wonderful qualities we ought to integrate into our marriage relationships, "*Put on therefore, as the elect of God, holy and beloved, bowels of mercies, kindness, humbleness of mind, meekness, longsuffering; Forbearing one another, and forgiving one another, if any man have a quarrel against any: even as Christ forgave you, so also do ye. And above all these things put on charity, which is the bond of perfectness.*"

In every relationship of life, especially in marriage, there will be times of problems and pressures that can eat at or literally destroy that relationship. Perhaps right now you are struggling in your marriage. As I share these seven keys that can transform your marriage, let me ask you to pray for a receptive heart and allow God to change you in the areas that need changing. In verse 14 it says to *"put on charity"* which indicates it is a choice, just as you *choose* to "put on" a coat. Let's use an acrostic for charity and "put on" these things:

C—Communication

In a survey among professional marriage counselors the number one problem they hear is: "My husband never talks with me." There is a lack of communication! Most men are lousy at communication, and this results in bitterness, fear, loneliness, failure, rebellion, or a sense of rejection. Men usually "clam up" or "blow up." But women are relational and need communication with their husbands! It has been said to "communicate or disintegrate." Learn to talk to each other. Learn to truly listen to your wife. Learn to share your heart with her. Learn to save your best heart energy for when you are together.

One way to improve in this area is to plan a time to communicate where you share ideas, goals, desires, plans, interests, and problems. Also, plan times just to listen to your wife's interests and look her in the eyes seeking to understand her heart and life. Remember, *communicate or disintegrate!*

H—Hugs

Now, maybe you are not into hugging. You say you are not the type to demonstrate a lot of physical affection. Well, it is time to change and break those chains of withdrawal and disconnectedness! First of all, it is good for you. Scientific tests reveal that regular hugging will add several years to your life! Second, it is not nearly as difficult to express physical affection as you probably think it is. And third, your family needs this from you about as much as they need anything else you can provide.

Do it for yourself and for your wife! It is reported that every woman needs at least eight hugs a day! Now, that is not an excuse to go around hugging every other woman. That could lead to big trouble! Save your hugs for your own wife, and make sure she gets plenty of them.

Hugging is a way of showing and sharing affection! Genesis 2:24 says, *"Therefore shall a man leave his father and his mother, and shall cleave* (stick to like glue) *unto his wife: and they shall be one flesh."* We are to hold fast, cling to our wives! *Hugs are healthy!*

A—Attention

Give time and effort to each other. Date regularly. My wife and I try to date once a week!

I once read the following joke: A couple was celebrating their Golden Wedding Anniversary, and a man asked, "What is the secret to your long marriage?" "Well," answered the husband, "we take time to go out for dinner twice a week. A little candlelight dinner, soft music, and a slow walk home. She goes on Tuesdays and I go on Fridays." That is not what we are talking about here!

Show interest in one another's hobbies, recreational activities, and personal interests. Spend time together, share duties, serve together in a ministry at church, and show interest in each other's lives by asking questions. You will not have a healthy marriage relationship without time and attention. Relationships only develop one way—through time together. *Attention takes intention!*

R—Responsibility

Someone said that marriage is like a midnight phone call. You get a ring and then you wake up! The marriage relationship carries many responsibilities with it that are not always evident when you are saying your vows.

Statistics indicate that divorce seldomly occurs in China. A young man asked a Chinese young man why this was. He explained, "I did not see my bride until I met her at the altar. My parents arranged the marriage." Then he was asked by the American young man, "What about falling in love and romance?" The Chinese young man answered, "That is the problem with marriages in America. You look upon it as romance. We look upon it as commitment and responsibility."

While there is nothing wrong with enjoying the romance in marriage, we must also commit to the responsibilities of the relationship. In the Scriptures, wives are taught to submit, reverence and honor the husband, to be a true help-meet. The husband is taught in the same passage in Ephesians 5 that he is to love with a self-sacrificing love; to nourish by giving leadership in the spiritual, emotional, and material realm; and to cherish his wife, which means to soften with warmth or be the protector. I believe that if we as husbands would care for our wives in this manner, we would see "a little bit of heaven on earth" in our homes! *Responsibility is reasonable!*

I—Intimacy

The word *intimacy* comes from the Latin word *intimus* which means the most personal, private area of the relationship, and this includes but is much bigger than physical, sexual intimacy. Our society has such a distorted view of and places such a great emphasis on physical sex, and yet true intimacy is missing in most marriages.

Intimacy is like a two-sided coin—it is exclusive and inclusive. It excludes improper relationships with others, while it focuses diligently on "just the two of us!"

In the book *The Bond of Intimacy,* the author, Ed Wheat, lists the following ways of developing true intimacy:

Physical touch/affection—non-sexual
Shared feelings
Closeness without inhibitions
Open communication and honesty
Spiritual harmony
Similar values held
Imparted secrets
Genuine understanding
Mutual confidence
Sense of warmth, safety, relaxation together
Sexual pleasures lovingly shared
Signs of love freely given and received
Mutual responsibility and caring
Abiding trust

Marriages are made in Heaven, but maintenance occurs in an earthly setting. It takes knowledge and patience. In the Old Testament, the Lord allowed one year for newlyweds to establish patterns of intimacy. Intimacy is simply touching one another—physically, emotionally, mentally, and spiritually. Reach out and touch the one you love. *Intimacy is touching!*

T—Tenderness

We tend to be so cruel and inconsiderate sometimes to the ones we love the most. With others we are kind, considerate, and tactful. There is something wrong with that picture! If you are treating coworkers and strangers with more sensitivity and thoughtfulness than you are giving your wife, you are headed for disaster.

Author Ed Wheat, in his book *Love Life,* states that there are four ways we hurt one another: words, looks, attitudes, and actions. What we really need in our relationships is: B-E-S-T. This is the prescription for a superb marriage:

Blessing. Speak kind and gracious words! Colossians 4:6 says, *"Let your speech be alway with grace, seasoned with salt...."* Express thankfulness and appreciation. And sometimes we need to just be quiet and patient!

Edifying. Build one another up. Don't tear each other down! First Corinthians 8:1 says, *"...charity edifieth."*

Sharing. Share in all areas of life—embrace the interests and desires of your spouse.

Touching. Tender touching says, "I care for you!" Show tender loving care!

Tenderness will transform!

Y—Yieldedness

Yieldedness literally deals with being submissive. Today everyone is crying out, "I've got my rights." How often we fight for our selfish preferences in things that really don't matter at all. These are petty pride struggles—something like a sibling rivalry. Yet in Ephesians 5:21 we are instructed, *"Submitting yourselves one to another in the fear of God."*

We are a self-centered society. Instead we need to be yielded in our relationships. We need to show mutual respect. Be agreeable, not argumentative. Gladly give up your way to prefer and please your spouse. Philippians 4:5 says, *"Let your moderation be known unto all men. The Lord is at hand."*

The key to being truly yielded and submissive is found in Ephesians 5:18–21:

Be not drunk with wine, wherein is excess; but be filled with the Spirit; Speaking to yourselves in psalms and hymns and spiritual songs, singing and making melody in your heart to the Lord; Giving thanks always for all things unto God and the Father in the name of our Lord Jesus Christ; Submitting yourselves one to another in the fear of God.

The more under the control of the Holy Spirit you are, the more you will be able to yield and submit your selfish will to the needs of your wife. *Yieldedness has no rights!*

Remember in Colossians 3:14 Paul said, " *And above all these things put on charity, which is the bond of perfectness.*" All of the wonderful actions and attitudes we render are to be clothed with charity. Take these seven keys from the word *charity* and apply them in your marriage relationship.

Solomon gave us a great truth and some words of encouragement in Song of Solomon 8:6–7, "*Set me as a seal upon thine heart, as a seal upon thine arm: for love is strong as death; jealousy is cruel as the grave: the coals thereof are coals of fire, which hath a most vehement flame. Many waters cannot quench love, neither can the floods drown it: if a man would give all the substance of his house for love, it would utterly be contemned.*" The flame of love in a healthy and biblical marriage relationship may have many trials and challenges. However, no matter what comes, this love cannot be drowned out.

Will you join me in making this fifth commitment of biblical manhood? Will you be faithful to your wedding vow—not only to abstain from extramarital affairs, but also to truly and deeply embrace and love the wife that God has given to you? Will you renew your commitment to truly love her, meet her needs, and be intimate and affectionate toward her? Keep the "honey" in the ongoing honeymoon with the wife God has given you, and as you work at developing your marriage, it will become stronger and more wonderfully blessed. God will greatly bless your home as you step up and take the spiritual leadership and the responsibility to love your wife the way Christ loves the church.

Summary

So, what have we learned?

C	Communicate or disintegrate.
H	Hugs are healthy.
A	Attention takes intention.
R	Responsibility is reasonable.
I	Intimacy is touching.
T	Tenderness will transform.
Y	Yieldedness has no rights.

Action Steps

Here are three **Action Steps** you can take to strengthen your marriage. (Initial and date when completed.)

1. Specifically and regularly pray for God's strength in strengthening your relationship with your wife.

   x_____   Date_____

2. Plan and make a list of definite ways you can more effectively minister to your wife.

   x_____   Date_____

3. Ask your wife what you can do as a spiritual leader to minister to her needs.

   x_____   Date_____

The Children God Has Given Me

Realizing that true revival begins with the hearts of fathers being turned to their children, I am determined to be the kind of father to my children that I have always yearned to have (Luke 1:17). This includes proper instruction, proper discipline, and proper family time together.

CHAPTER EIGHT

Growing My Children for God's Glory

T he subject of growing our children for God's glory demands our utmost attention. So many children in today's homes are growing up without the right kind of father. I read an article recently in a major newspaper which stated that every night forty percent of American children will go to bed in homes in which their fathers do not live.

Three challenging and nearly epidemic scenarios face families today. The first is a single parent home in which no dad is present and the mother must assume the fatherly role. The second is a home in which the birth father is not present and a stepfather must assume the role of father, but often the mother will not allow the stepdad to fulfill this role. The third unfortunate situation is that a dad is present, but he will not assume his role as father or the responsibilities of fatherhood but instead plays a passive role.

In this chapter, I want to help and encourage you to be the right kind of father. I recognize that you may have one of those three scenarios in your own home. I do not write these words to shame or guilt you over the mistakes of the past—but rather to challenge you to step up and be the father that God desires you to be from this point forward.

God desires a generation of godly children to be raised in this world today. Yet, so many fathers fail. We fail to know God as our own Father; we fail to nurture our children; and we fail to pass on our faith to the next generation. Even Eli, the priest in 1 Samuel 2–3, ruined his home and lost his sons because he failed to give them the right instruction and the right influence, and he restrained them not. This was God's analysis of Israel's priest—their spiritual leader. God's Word makes it clear that the primary responsibility for rearing children rests with you—the father—for you are the head of your home.

Ephesians 6:4 states, *"And, ye fathers, provoke not your children to wrath: but bring them up in the nurture and admonition of the Lord."* This verse presents three key thoughts about fathering, and remember, this is not some experimental secular philosophy—it is the Word of the Perfect Father!

These are God's instructions through the Apostle Paul. Notice, it says, *"…bring them up."* This is not passive but active, for we are to *"Train up a child in the way he should go…"* (Proverbs 22:6). This denotes deliberate, positive action for raising children, as it doesn't just happen by itself. Observe that it is also a command to be followed, not a suggestion to be considered. It is to be followed just as any other command from Scripture. It is also a present, continuous activity denoting an ongoing, continual process. Galatians 6:9 says, *"And let us not be weary in well doing: for in due season we shall reap, if we faint not."* Don't allow apathy and indifference to detour you from your God-given responsibility of child-rearing. Let's look at the three aspects of this command.

Don't Provoke Them

This means don't rouse them to wrath or exasperate them. Children can be provoked or stirred up to the point of anger, frustration, and bitterness if we fail to deal with them properly. Children, teens, and even young adults are fragile. Don't "take the wind out of their sails." As a parent, particularly as a father, you can provoke your child to wrath by the following:

1. Inconsistency and hypocrisy. Our lives before others may appear genuine, warm, and considerate. Yet at home with your children, you are transformed into a person who loses his temper, uses foul language, practices sinful habits, watches corrupt TV shows or videos, and shows no personal walk with Christ. *Your walk talks louder than your talk talks!* This is a BIG source of anger and resentment in our children!

2. A lack of praise for their efforts. We are quick to point out their faults or when they are wrong about something, but we fail to commend the good in their lives. Consider having a formula of ten to one—ten positive, affirming times to every one negative word of correction or discipline. Your children will respond very well to your words of encouragement and affirmation.

3. Abusive verbal attacks. Degrading statements and harsh tones are often used when trying to correct disobedience in our children. Rather than dealing with them in firm but compassionate Spirit-led tones, we fly off the handle with harshness and irritation. Ask the Lord to help you control your spirit and your tongue.

4. Failing to allow open, free communication. We don't allow children to freely give their thoughts on matters. We don't ask questions to show interest or to share in their problems and frustrations. Often we "shush" them or suppress them rather than let them speak respectfully but openly. When our children come to us with the right spirit, they should find a listening ear and an understanding heart.

5. Making promises, then failing to keep them. Our children remember the promises we make, and they lose trust in us when we don't keep them. You might consider just asking your child if there is any promise you have made that you haven't kept. Then determine to follow through!

6. Not making time to enjoy our children. We need to have "family times" regularly. Your children need quantity and quality time with you, and this must be a priority in your weekly schedule.

7. Failing to admit when we are wrong. Be open, honest and transparent. Be willing to admit when you have blown it. Be willing to apologize and ask forgiveness from your child. This builds a child's trust and will cause children to open up.

A child's view of his earthly father often creates his attitude and his view of his Heavenly Father. *"Fathers, provoke not your children to wrath."* Thank God for a Heavenly Father who is always there, ready to listen, eager to forgive, and gracious to provide. Notice the second mandate.

Train Them

"…bring them up in the nurture…of the Lord." The word *nurture* includes the training of a child.

Training is preventative. It commands, exhorts, and instructs. It shows children the path of behavior (which way to go).

Training is corrective. It reproves, rebukes, and corrects. It helps children change their behavior and put away wrong attitudes and actions. This is what molds godly character.

Training is disciplinary. It uses the biblical pattern for the purpose of bringing about change, Proverbs 29:15–17, *"The rod and reproof give wisdom: but a child left to himself bringeth his mother to shame. When the wicked are multiplied, transgression increaseth: but the righteous shall see their fall. Correct thy son, and he shall give thee rest; yea, he shall give delight unto thy soul."*

Many Christian parents have become humanistic in their thinking because of the influence of what they feel, read, or hear. Proverbs 22:15 reads, *"Foolishness is bound in the heart of a child; but the rod of correction shall drive it far from him."* I am not speaking of abuse or inappropriate physical discipline. Proper biblical use of the rod by following these steps will bring about amazing change in the heart! Please consider following these simple steps when disciplining your child.

1. Get your heart right first—don't discipline in anger.
2. Get alone with the child.
3. Deal biblically with particular sin (lying, disrespect, etc.).
4. Tell them the number of swats according to action.
5. Teach them to cry quietly and not to struggle.
6. Use a flat object other than your hand.
7. Test the sting of your "swat" on yourself first.
8. After the swats, immediately embrace your child.
9. Speak of your love and let your child cry on your shoulder.
10. Soothe the sting and comfort the heart.
11. After the tears, kneel and pray together.
12. Speak to God of your love for your child.
13. Let your child pray to confess sin to God.
14. Embrace and show affection.

Don't end your discipline session until your child's heart is open to you and tender once again. If you follow these steps and your child is still closed and angry in spirit toward you, something is wrong and you must seek to understand and to resolve it. It may mean that you misunderstood or that your child feels you were unfair or unwilling to listen. Whatever the case, restore your child's heart to yourself before you finish.

Biblical, loving discipline will accomplish much in your child's heart!

Teach Them

One of the great problems and sins in our homes is that fathers fail to give "admonition" or teaching from the Word. Ninety-eight percent of Christian homes do not have regular family Bible devotions. *Teach* means "to put in mind."

> *Hear, ye children, the instruction of a father, and attend to know understanding. For I give you good doctrine, forsake ye not my law. For I was my father's son, tender and only beloved in the sight of my mother. He taught me also, and said unto me, Let thine heart retain my words: keep my commandments, and live. Get wisdom, get understanding: forget it not; neither decline from the words of my mouth.*
> —PROVERBS 4:1–5

Verse 1 says, "*Hear, ye children, the instruction of a father,*" but where are the *fathers*? They are missing in today's culture. They are losing out on the blessings for their children, and they are in direct disobedience to God's commands! How can our children hear our instruction if we aren't giving it? Television, public education, and peers are teaching our children, but fathers are not!

Father, family devotions will transform your home. Bring up your children in the admonition of the Lord. Set a definite time for devotions. Be consistent—don't miss this time. Make it practical and fun. "*...Fathers, provoke not your children to wrath: but bring them up in the nurture and admonition of the Lord.*"

Having had the responsibility to raise five children, I can truly attest that these three key principles are vitally important. Fathers, we have no excuse for failing to do our job. If God has given you a child, He has given you a command to bring up that child for Him.

Some years ago, at a large fair in Dallas, Texas, an interesting, yet tragic exhibition took place. A sallow-faced, emaciated boy was showing a prize-winning hog. The boy's hair was unkempt and matted. His disposition and vocabulary were vulgar. He was smoking one cigarette after another. The owner of the prize-winning hog was the father of this boy. The father had been a success at raising hogs but a dismal failure at raising a son.

Thank God for fathers who see their primary calling, occupation, and ministry to be that of raising godly children for God's glory and who invest their time and energies into their families.

Today there are three popular methods of raising children. One is called "The Permissive Plan" which is a product of the religion of humanism. This philosophy teaches to let your child do as he or she wishes. It says, "Don't repress your child in any way, or you may warp them. Every child has rights." This is our basic educational system's philosophy.

The second approach is "The Repressive Plan" which carries the idea that we must beat our children into submission and humiliate them. Mark Twain humorously said that when a child is born, put that child in a box with a small hole in the top; and when that child becomes a teen, plug up the hole. That idea is humorous, yes, but sadly wrong. Yet some homes use a repressive plan that resembles this approach.

The third approach is called "Trial and Error." This is the approach used by most families—even Christian families. This approach says, "If things are going okay, we must be doing things right. If we run into problems we will change, try something else, and hope for the best. We have no guarantee that our plans will work and that our children will turn out right." This approach to child-rearing is both experimental and faithless. It creates inconsistency and unpredictability in the home and actually teaches the children a spirit of pragmatism that will follow them long into their adult life.

I understand that children and young people have minds of their own and eventually they will be responsible for their own actions, but may I challenge you to follow this fourth plan, "God's Divine Plan" which we have already seen. This is the faith-based approach that God still blesses!

A story is told of a father who took his little boy on his knee and told him the story of the lost sheep. "One day one of the shepherd's favorite sheep found a hole in the fence and crawled through. The sheep was glad to be freed from the confines of the sheep fold. As he ran and skipped in the sunshine he wandered as far away as he could. As he wandered he got caught in a thorny bush with his wool. Night came and all of a sudden the cry of a wolf was heard. Upon spying the entangled sheep, the wolf began to nip and bite the sheep. Finally the shepherd appeared and rescued the poor frightened sheep that was dirty, exhausted, and injured. The shepherd brought the sheep back to the safety of the sheepfold."

The little boy listened intently with tears in his eyes and he asked his father, "Daddy, did the shepherd nail up the hole in the fence?"

I have watched, observed, and studied the lives of precious young people to whom I have ministered over the past forty years. Without fail, when young people find themselves going the wrong direction in their lives it is usually because there has been a hole in the fence somewhere. Father, will you determine to plug up the hole in the fence and strengthen the protection of your sheepfold? Heed God's commands, lest one of your precious sheep wanders away into danger. Take a moment now and embrace this sixth commitment as a godly man!

Summary

In this chapter we saw three important aspects of growing our children for God's glory.

1. Don't Provoke Them
2. Do Discipline Them
3. Do Teach Them

Action Steps

Here are three **Action Steps** you can take to become the father God has directed you to be. (Initial and date when completed.)

1. Make sure your personal life and walk reflect a godly example your children can follow, and make a simple list of some "holes" in your fence.

   x_____   Date_____

2. Determine to establish and maintain a constant family devotion time no matter how difficult it may be.

   x_____   Date_____

3. Write out on a 3 x 5 card and memorize Ephesians 6:4 and Colossians 3:21.

   x_____   Date_____

Purity in Life

Realizing the reprobate society in which we live,
I am determined by the help of God to remain
pure from sexual sin, fleeing from youthful lusts
(2 Timothy 2:22), and thinking only on those
things which are honoring to the
Lord Jesus Christ (Philippians 4:8).

Separation from the World

Realizing that God has commanded us to be
separated (2 Corinthians 6:14–18) and that He
has told us not to be conformed to this world
(Romans 12:2), I have determined to separate myself
from worldly amusements, from intimate fellowship
with things or persons in the world that would pull
me away from these commitments to Christ, and from
other Christians who would determine not to walk
in accordance with the Word of God.

CHAPTER NINE

Pursuing a Pure and Godly Life and Yielding Myself to Be Separated from the World

I will cover two commitments in this chapter that are very closely related—pursuing purity in my life and separating myself from the world.

Traveling through this life, men face a constant pull from the world with all of its glitter and glamour, and our flesh finds all that surrounds us so appealing. Through the corridors of time, men have faced worldly attractions but never before as in this time. With today's technology, we find every imaginable toy and temptation at our fingertips, calling us to be drawn toward the world.

We live in a hedonistic, humanistic, and materialistic society which tells us to indulge, enjoy, and fulfill those fleshly appetites and to live for personal pleasure.

James speaks of this conflict in chapter 4:1–3, "*From whence come wars and fightings among you? come they not hence, even of your lusts that war in your members? Ye lust, and have not: ye kill, and desire to have, and cannot obtain: ye fight and war, yet ye have not, because ye ask not. Ye ask, and receive not, because ye ask amiss, that ye may consume it upon your lusts.*" Then James clearly tells us that our alignment and involvement in the world shows our unfaithfulness to the One to whom we are to be committed in verse 4, "*Ye adulterers and adulteresses, know ye not that the friendship of the world is enmity with God? whosoever therefore will be a friend of the world is the enemy of God.*"

God clearly spells out that a godly man is to live separated from the world. One old timer stated years ago, "I don't smoke and I don't chew, and I don't go with the girls who do."

Biblical separation from the world is being as close to the Lord as you can and staying as far away from the world as possible. Ed Cole said, "Manhood and Christlikeness are synonymous." John the Beloved said in 1 John 2:15–16, "*Love not the world, neither the things that are in the world. If any man love the world, the love of the Father is not in him. For all that is in the world, the lust of the flesh, and the lust of the eyes, and the pride of life, is not of the Father, but is of the world.*"

Your goal should be to love the Lord God with all your heart, with all your soul, and with all your mind (Matthew 22:37). You are also to seek things above and set your affections on things above, "*If ye then be risen with Christ, seek those things which are above, where Christ sitteth on the right hand of God. Set your affection on things above, not on things on the earth*" (Colossians 3:1–2).

You are setting your affection on things above when you are faithful in prayer, reading the Word, and to your local church, as discussed in previous chapters.

However, we do have an enemy and an adversary who will continually attempt to draw us away into the world. This enemy is Satan. We are warned of him, and we are to stand against him bearing God's armor.

Be sober, be vigilant; because your adversary the devil, as a roaring lion, walketh about, seeking whom he may devour:—1 Peter 5:8

Finally, my brethren, be strong in the Lord, and in the power of his might. Put on the whole armour of God, that ye may be able to stand against the wiles of the devil. For we wrestle not against flesh and blood, but against principalities, against powers, against the rulers of the darkness of this world, against spiritual wickedness in high places. Wherefore take unto you the whole armour of God, that ye may be able to withstand in the evil day, and having done all, to stand.—Ephesians 6:10–13

We need to be aware that there are doors in our lives through which Satan can make inroads to draw us into the world and worldly pleasures. We must keep those doors locked. In our homes we use special locks, dead bolts, alarm systems, bars on windows, and watch dogs. Many of us will go to great extremes to secure our homes, but we leave the doors of our minds wide open.

Just as you would lock up your home when you leave for the day or go to bed at night—even so you must guard your heart and life from Satan's tactics. Your mind is a valued trophy over which a fierce battle is being constantly waged. The Apostle Paul likens the mind to a citadel or a stronghold where a strategic war is being waged. Notice in 2 Corinthians 10:3–5, *"For though we walk in the flesh, we do not war after the flesh: (For the weapons of our warfare are not carnal, but mighty through God to the pulling down of strong holds;) Casting down imaginations, and every high thing that exalteth itself against the knowledge of God, and bringing into captivity every thought to the obedience of Christ."* Our minds are referred to here as our imaginations, knowledge, and thoughts.

God wants control of your mind because He wants you! You *are* what you *think*! Proverbs 23:7, *"For as he thinketh in his heart so is he…."* Someone has said, "Sow a thought and you reap a deed. Sow a deed and you reap a habit. Sow a habit and you reap a character. Sow a character and you reap a destiny." The whole process begins in the area of the thoughts—in the mind.

Satan's Desire

> *And the Lord said, Simon, Simon, behold, Satan hath desired to have you, that he may sift you as wheat:*
> —LUKE 22:31

Satan wants your mind. He wants to capture, control, and corrupt your mind. The devil knows he can disgrace the testimony of a sincere Christian man if he can capture the control center—his mind. If he can get you to *think* wrong, he can subtly lead you to *do* wrong. The enemy is aware that God destroyed an entire civilization because of "evil imaginations" (Genesis 6:5–7).

Satan's Devices

> *Lest Satan should get an advantage of us: for we are not ignorant of his devices.*—2 CORINTHIANS 2:11

Satan has a well laid strategy. It is a two-pronged attack, and it is formidable and powerful.

He blinds the minds of the unsaved. Second Corinthians 4:3–4 says, *"But if our gospel be hid, it is hid to them that are lost: In whom the god of this world hath blinded the minds of them which believe not, lest the light of the glorious gospel of Christ, who is the image of God, should shine unto them."* Spiritually blinded minds cannot see or understand spiritual truth. John 3:3 says, *"…Except a man be born again, he cannot see the kingdom of God."* Whether it is someone who claims to be an agnostic, or simply rejects the Gospel, we need to share the Gospel and pray for those who are spiritually blind. It is through hearing the Gospel that darkness is destroyed. The Gospel is light!

He corrupts the minds of the saved. Second Corinthians 11:3 says, *"But I fear, lest by any means, as the serpent beguiled Eve through his subtilty, so your minds should be corrupted from the simplicity that is in Christ."* Don't think that salvation means automatic immunity from satanic attack of your mind. Saints across this world are filled with anxieties, fears, doubts, impure thoughts, cares, worries, false doctrines, and bitterness. Beware of Satan's devices—he is attempting to corrupt your mind if you are a child of God.

Satan's Doors

> *Wherefore gird up the loins of your mind, be sober, and hope to the end for the grace that is to be brought unto you at the revelation of Jesus Christ; As obedient children, not fashioning yourselves according to the former lusts in your ignorance: But as he which hath called you is holy, so be ye holy in all manner of conversation; Because it is written, Be ye holy; for I am holy.* —1 PETER 1:13–16

How is Satan able to corrupt our minds? The security is not tight enough! He comes through unguarded and unlocked doors. Even the Great Wall of China failed to keep out its enemy because one bribed gatekeeper let in the enemy. Here are several doors through which Satan can corrupt a mind.

Unconfessed sin. Unconfessed and harbored sin in anyone's life is the devil's open door. Ephesians 4:26–27 says, *"Be ye angry, and sin not: let not the sun go down upon your wrath: Neither give place to the devil."* Don't allow a day to end with unconfessed sin in your life. If you do so, you give Satan an open door. That sin lies there and like a cancer, it begins to grow and spread. It affects your attitude with anger, bitterness, wrath, and malice. It influences you to wrong actions and a wrong lifestyle!

The answer is *repentance*—a change of mind regarding your sin. Five of the seven churches in Revelation 2 and 3 were told to repent! Sin must be uprooted and removed. First John 1:9 says, *"If we confess our sins, he is faithful and just to forgive us our sins, and to cleanse us from all unrighteousness."* Confession provides cleansing and brings revival! Why is it that we tolerate and allow sin? Come to Christ with a soft heart and confess your sins today!

Undisciplined thoughts. In the lives of many Christian men, this door is left wide open. We need to actively guard our minds and keep them from wandering. Solomon warned in Proverbs 4:23, *"Keep thy heart with all diligence; for out of it are the issues of life."*

Keep your mind! Guard it! Control it! If you become passive in your thought life and don't guard every thought, a wrong thought will be planted in your mind. Having wrong friends, wrong counsel, or worldly amusement can lead to passivity. Many Christian men do not exercise much control over what they feed their minds. Television, videos, video games, the internet, rock music, country music, and even commercials can bring wrong thoughts into our minds.

The answer is *resistance*. James 4:7 says, *"Submit yourselves therefore to God. Resist the devil, and he will flee from you."* Say "no" to sin, whether it be through TV, music, movies, magazines, books, or the computer. You must choose to resist! Resist the enemy in the name of Jesus Christ. Satan has no right or authority over your mind or body—they belong to Christ.

Uncontrolled appetites. Today is the day of the free use of drugs (downers/uppers), alcohol, pornography, and even food! There is tragic abuse of one or more of these areas, leaving wide open the door to destruction of both the mind and the body. The AMA chairman, Dr. Marvin Block said, "Ours is a drug-oriented society." This is largely because alcohol has become a socially acceptable habit. It is rarely thought of as a drug, but it is a scientific fact that it is a drug.

The answer is **renewal.** If your mind has been damaged by drugs, liquor, pornography, or other sin, then it must be renewed and rebuilt by God's power. Ephesians 4:23 says, *"And be renewed in the spirit of your mind."* Romans 12:2 says, *"And be not conformed to this world: but be ye transformed by the renewing of your mind, that ye may prove what is that good, and acceptable, and perfect, will of God."* This process of renewal takes time, prayer, patience, spiritual training, and God's Word!

Uncommitted cares. Our society is complex and filled with stress and pressure from every side—work, family, and finances. It is very easy to become despondent, discouraged, and defeated when we allow ourselves to dwell on negative situations or problems. If you look long enough, you will find plenty about which to get depressed. Millions of men live in a world of depression. God says in 1 Peter 5:7 that we are to cast all of our care upon Him! He doesn't intend for us to carry these burdens and dwell under the weight of life's pressure.

The answer is **remembrance.** Philippians 4:8 says, *"Finally, brethren, whatsoever things are true, whatsoever things are honest, whatsoever things are just, whatsoever things are pure, whatsoever things are lovely, whatsoever things are of good report; if there be any virtue, and if there be any praise, think on these things."* God designed the mind to be able to think on only one thing at a time, so if you keep your mind on the right things you won't have problems thinking about the wrong things! Start each day with reading the Bible, and choose to think on what you read throughout the day! Isaiah 26:3 reads, *"Thou wilt keep him in perfect peace, whose mind is stayed on thee: because he trusteth in thee."*

These four doors are Satan's doors of opportunity to draw you into worldly and wicked activities which will defeat you and ruin your testimony for the Lord. Paul said in Ephesians 4:27, *"Neither give place to the devil."* Don't give him any ground or territory in your mind or life. Determine to stand fast in the Lord. Keep your doors locked and guard the entrances to your mind!

Your faithful and consistent walk with the Lord will strengthen and encourage others; however, when you backslide and get into the world, your life will have the opposite effect on others, especially your family and friends. I once heard a true story that illustrates this fact.

Five mountain climbers were experienced and equipped for their climb to the top of Mt. Blanc in the Himalayan Mountains. The first day's climb took these five men over the jagged and rocky terrain on the lower part of the mountain. On the second day, they were already working their way up the slick and sheer wall of the glacier. The five men were spaced apart by about fifty feet. A safety rope connected all five men so that in the event one would lose his footing, the others could keep him from falling.

In an unsuspecting moment the lead climber carelessly miscalculated his footing and began to slide down the face of the glacier. The other four climbers were unprepared, and as the lead man went cascading by, each of the remaining men was jerked from his position, and all five went sliding down, landing on the jagged rocks.

This story is repeated over and over again each day as careless Christians who are climbing up the mountain to victory in their Christian lives take their eyes off the Lord, lose their footing, and begin to backslide. We never fall alone! We always end up carrying others along with us—dragging them to destruction. Ephesians 5:15 challenges us, *"See then that ye walk circumspectly...."* Oh, the pinnacle from which many Christians have fallen and the depths to which they have sunk!

Will you embrace the seventh and eighth commitments of godly manhood? Will you choose purity and separation in a world that is filled with sin and vice? This will be one of your biggest battles. Satan is relentless, but God's grace is greater! First John 4:4 says, *"Ye are of God, little children, and have overcome them: because greater is he that is in you, than he that is in the world."*

Summary

In this chapter we have been warned of:

1. Satan's Desire
2. Satan's Devices
3. Satan's Doors

Action Steps

Here are three **Action Steps** you can take to become separated from the world. (Initial and date when completed.)

1. With what doors do you struggle the most in your life? List them, and write out a plan to lock those doors.

   x_____   Date_____

2. One of the keys to victory is memorizing the Word of God. On a 3 x 5 card write out and memorize Romans 12:1–2.

   x_____   Date_____

3. What object, place, person, or activity draws you the most quickly into the world? Make a decision to avoid it.

   x_____   Date_____

Reaching Other Men for the Master

Realizing that God has called me to be His ambassador (2 Corinthians 5:20) I will do all I can to reach others with the Gospel through my soulwinning efforts. I will also do my utmost to invite and encourage others to visit my church where they can hear the Gospel, thereby partially fulfilling the Great Commission.

CHAPTER TEN

Reaching Others
for the Master
Ephesians 6:19

If we desire to have hearts for God and to obediently follow Him, then reaching others for Christ must be a part of our daily lives. The heart of our Saviour was *"to seek and to save that which was lost"* (Luke 19:10). Jesus also told His disciples, Peter and Andrew, in Matthew 4:19, *"…Follow me, and I will make you fishers of men."* It has been rightly said that if you are not fishing for men, you are not following Christ.

Having been born in Oregon and raised in a small logging community, I have enjoyed the sport of fishing from a very early age. I grew up spending time along the Lacreal Creek and caught many a fine trout in those days. Today I have in my garage some fine fishing equipment with all of the accessories. Yet over these last forty plus years, that equipment has been seldom used. The fish are still out there, but for a variety of reasons I have not made the effort to go after them.

Even so, there are many men who may have gone after the souls of men at one time, but for a long time they have failed to go fishing for men—though they have all of the basic tools and equipment.

During my fishing days, there was nothing more refreshing and exciting than hooking a nice, big German brown trout, fighting him in, and then landing him in the boat or on the shore. Likewise, one of the greatest experiences and joys of a Christian man's life is to have the thrill of seeing a lost sinner saved and ultimately seeing him land on Heaven's shore!

We have a variety of excuses and reasons why we don't go fishing for men, but they will be empty and hollow one day when we stand before our Master. What are some excuses that keep a man from soulwinning—from taking the wonderful message of eternal life to lost souls?

Fear keeps us from reaching the lost. "I'm too fearful to talk to folks about the Gospel." Many men will confess that they have used this reason to keep them from soulwinning and giving out the Gospel. We have no problem talking with others about any and every other subject imaginable, but even godly men experience a real measure of fear in soulwinning.

Even the Apostle Paul, an ardent, faithful soulwinner, who had the joy of leading scores of souls to faith in Christ, asked for prayer for boldness in Ephesians 6:19, *"And for me, that utterance may be given unto me, that I may open my mouth boldly, to make known the mystery of the gospel."* Pray for boldness, and the Lord will help you. You may fear rejection—that those you witness to will reject the Gospel—but be mindful of the fact that the one they are rejecting is Christ, not you.

A lack of knowledge keeps us from reaching the lost. Another reason men fail to go soulwinning is that they feel they are inadequate in their knowledge of the Scriptures or that they lack the skill to present the Gospel properly. We can always improve upon our knowledge of the Word and develop our ability to present the wonderful message of the Gospel more effectively. However, never lose sight of the fact that it is not our knowledge of the Bible or even our skill in presenting the Gospel that matters as much as the power of the Word. *"For the word of God is quick, and powerful, and sharper than any twoedged sword, piercing even to the dividing asunder of soul and spirit, and of the joints and marrow, and is a discerner of the thoughts and intents of the heart"* (Hebrews 4:12).

We also need the working of the Holy Spirit, *"And when he is come, he will reprove the world of sin, and of righteousness, and of judgment"* (John 16:8). Ultimately we need to understand that we can save no one—this is God's doing. We are only responsible to present the message, and it is God who saves the sinner.

Busyness keeps us from reaching the lost. We live in a busy world, and many men use the excuse of not having time for soulwinning. Every person has been given the same amount of time in a day, and often, a lack of soulwinnning is not an issue of enough time, but misplaced priorities. We need to change our priorities and make time to go soulwinning.

Soulwinning should become part of your lifestyle—you should be always ready to give out a tract, invite someone to church, or present the Gospel. Peter said it most pointedly in 1 Peter 3:15, *"But sanctify the Lord God in your hearts: and be ready always to give an answer to every man that asketh you a reason of the hope that is in you with meekness and fear."*

As mentioned before, we may feel inadequate to present the Gospel, but the Gospel is very simple and can be presented in a variety of ways. The Gospel can be presented by sharing your testimony of how you trusted Christ as Saviour. Or, you could read through a good Gospel tract with someone and explain each point. Ask your pastor for some advice on other ways you can effectively give out the Gospel.

The truth is, all excuses can be overcome if you are truly willing to be obedient in engaging yourself in the great ministry of soulwinning.

How to Lead a Soul to Christ

Someone once said, "The fruit of a Christian is another Christian." There is much truth in that statement. Sometimes a person can be very active in sharing the Gospel but will not see much fruit. It is important to learn how to be *effective* in sharing the Gospel. Here are some truths that every soulwinner should remember as he prepares to help another soul spend an eternity with Christ:

A soulwinner should start with the truth of God's love for every individual. John 3:16 is perhaps the most familiar verse in all the New Testament, *"For God so loved the world, that he gave his only begotten Son, that whosoever believeth in him should not perish, but have everlasting life."* There are people who actually believe that God hates them and wants them to go to Hell because of their sin. A sinner will never accept a Saviour who he believes does not love him.

A soulwinner must emphasize the fact that we are all sinners —there are no exceptions. Some people understand God's "love," but they feel that a "loving" God would never send anyone to Hell. These sinners must also understand that the God of "love" is also first and foremost, a holy God. All men fall short of the holy standard He has set. Because we "fall short," we are condemned to an eternity in Hell (Romans 3:23).

A soulwinner must teach the sinner that his sin carries with it an expensive price tag. According to Romans 6:23, *"For the wages of sin is death...."* In Ezekiel 18:20, the Israelites learned of the price tag that sin carries, *"The soul that sinneth, it shall die. The son shall not bear the iniquity of the father, neither shall the father bear the iniquity of the son: the righteousness of the righteous shall be upon him, and the wickedness of the wicked shall be upon him."* John 3:36 speaks of the wrath of God that abides on a person who rejects Christ, *"He that believeth on the Son hath everlasting life: and he that believeth not the Son shall not see life; but the wrath of God abideth on him."*

A soulwinner should demonstrate the good news that Jesus has already paid this price. Romans 6:23 deals with the penalty of sin, but it also deals with the promise of salvation, "...*but the gift of God is eternal life through Jesus Christ our Lord.*" Romans 5:8 shows the sinner that Christ died for us while were yet sinners, "*But God commendeth his love toward us, in that, while we were yet sinners, Christ died for us.*"

A soulwinner must remember that a sinner must *personally* accept Christ as Saviour. Romans 10:13 promises, "*For whosoever shall call upon the name of the Lord shall be saved.*" A sinner may believe that God loves him, that he is a sinner, that Jesus died to pay his sin debt, and still be lost. The soulwinner should not seek a simple mental assent to a list of subscribed facts. The sinner must repent, confess, and fully believe in Christ, so he can then know the joy of being a Christian.

Ask the sinner, "Is there anything that would hinder you from trusting Christ right now, today, as your Saviour?" This question will show the soulwinner if there are still any "obstacles" that must be removed before a sinner trusts Christ. This statement also serves as a good transition into "drawing" the Gospel "net"—the sinner's salvation.

After a man is saved, part of the Great Commission is still unfulfilled. We are commanded to go, to win, to baptize, and to teach (disciple). An effective soulwinner will determine to see each aspect of the Great Commission come to fruition with those he leads to Christ.

If we will be effective in our soulwinning efforts, we should also understand that there are some important prerequisites to be an effective soulwinner.

The Effective Christian and His Witness

In John 15, Christ tells the disciples that if they would abide in Him, they would bear much fruit. John later stated, "*I have no greater joy than to hear that my children walk in truth*" (3 John 1:4). The only way John could have these "children" was by being a personal soulwinner. Here are some biblical prerequisites for being an effective Christian:

A soulwinner should have a proper life's objective. Matthew 6:33 admonishes us, *"...seek ye first the kingdom of God, and his righteousness; and all these things shall be added unto you."* The objectives of our lives should not be to "get ahead" in the rat race. Rather, we must be genuinely consumed with Kingdom living—living with eternity in mind.

A soulwinner must be willing to pay the price. According to 2 Timothy 2:3–4, a good soldier at times will endure hardness. The soulwinner will be called upon to make self-sacrifices, live a separated life, and possibly endure persecution.

A soulwinner must have a love for God's Word. Jeremiah, the weeping prophet, stated, *"...thy word was unto me the joy and rejoicing of mine heart..."* (Jeremiah 15:16). If we do not love the Word of God, we will have a difficult time sharing it with others.

A soulwinner should manifest a servant's heart. In Philippians 2:5–8, Paul admonishes the church to have the mind of Christ—the one who took upon Him the form of a servant.

> *"Let this mind be in you, which was also in Christ Jesus: Who, being in the form of God, thought it not robbery to be equal with God: But made himself of no reputation, and took upon him the form of a servant, and was made in the likeness of men: And being found in fashion as a man, he humbled himself, and became obedient unto death, even the death of the cross."*

A soulwinner must not trust his own flesh or abilities. Paul, while still writing to the church at Philippi, warned them of the danger of trusting, or placing one's confidence, in the flesh. If there was ever a person who had reason to trust his natural abilities, it was Paul. But Paul realized that without Christ, he could do nothing.

A soulwinner must avoid bitterness at all costs. The writer of Hebrews challenged the Jewish believers to avoid the root of bitterness for two reasons. First, it would harm their soulwinning endeavors. Second, many other believers would be defiled. *"Looking diligently lest any man fail of the grace of God; lest any root of bitterness springing up trouble you, and thereby many be defiled"* (Hebrews 12:15). It is unwise for a soulwinner to allow discouragement and bitterness into his life.

A soulwinner must lead a disciplined life. While writing to the carnal Corinthian Christians, Paul spoke of how an athlete has one goal—the victor's crown. An athlete will do whatever it takes to win that prize. He puts his body into a very regimented schedule and lives a disciplined life. Paul used that analogy to drive home the importance of discipline in a Christian's life.

These prerequisites are not rules; rather they reflect the attitude of a Spirit-filled soulwinner. Without them, we cannot be effective in reaching others for Christ.

As we faithfully go out and share the Gospel, God will bring forth the glorious results. When we give out the Gospel, God is glorified and His Kingdom is advanced. There is no greater motivation for a godly man to witness than that our Master might be glorified. First Corinthians 6:20 says, *"For ye are bought with a price: therefore glorify God in your body, and in your spirit, which are God's."* Another wonderful reason to share the Good News is that there is great joy in Heaven when one sinner is saved. Luke 15:7 says, *"I say unto you, that likewise joy shall be in heaven over one sinner that repenteth, more than over ninety and nine just persons, which need no repentance."* When one sinner repents and by faith receives Christ as Saviour, Heaven rejoices—this should cause us to rejoice.

The psalmist said that if we give out the Gospel with burdened and broken hearts, we will come back with great joy, having led someone to Christ, *"They that sow in tears shall reap in joy. He that goeth forth and weepeth, bearing precious seed, shall doubtless come again with rejoicing, bringing his sheaves with him"* (Psalm 126:5–6).

As we share the Gospel, we are giving others the greatest gift that could ever be given. Harriet Beecher said, "The greatest thing one human being can do for another human being is to win them to Jesus." There are also rewards in Heaven for the faithful soulwinner, as stated in Daniel 12:3, *"And they that be wise shall shine as the brightness of the firmament; and they that turn many to righteousness as the stars for ever and ever."* In 1 Thessalonians 2:19–20, Paul tells of a special crown awaiting the soulwinner, *"For what is our hope, or joy, or crown of rejoicing? Are not even ye in the presence of our Lord Jesus Christ at his coming? For ye are our glory and joy."* You and I would be wise to make soulwinning a practical part of our daily lives. We read in Proverbs 11:30, *"The fruit of the righteous is a tree of life; and he that winneth souls is wise."*

Many years ago, there was a great meeting of all the Salvation Army delegates. The highlight of the meeting was to be the final address by the great William Booth, the founder and director of the Salvation Army. All were waiting expectantly to hear from this great man of God. Finally, word arrived that General Booth would be unable to attend. There was great disappointment. However, he had sent a special message for all the delegates and those attending. What great message would be given? What stirring and challenging themes would he present? As the message was opened, the following words were read: "Members and friends at this great convention of the Salvation Army—OTHERS," and the spokesman sat down. There was total quietness and an air of shock.

Two thousand years ago, the God of Heaven came to this earth, was born, lived thirty-three years, died on a Cross, rose again three days later, and for forty more days walked this earth. But, just minutes before His leaving and ascension to Heaven, He left His final message in Acts 1:8, *"But ye shall receive power, after that the Holy Ghost is come upon you: and ye shall be witnesses unto me both in Jerusalem, and in all Judaea, and in Samaria, and unto the uttermost part of the earth."*

OTHERS—the last word with which Jesus left us. May we with boldness carry out His last request—to be His witnesses, to reach others.

Summary

In this chapter we have seen that a godly man is actively involved in reaching other men for the Master through soulwinning. We learned some key points about:

1. How to Lead a Soul to Christ
2. The Effective Christian and His Witness

Action Steps

Here are three **Action Steps** you can take to involve yourself in reaching others with the Gospel. (Initial and date when completed.)

1. Get a handful of Gospel tracts and carry them with you. Hand out a minimum of two tracts a day for a week.

   x_____   Date_____

2. Commit to go out weekly for a month through your church visitation program.

   x_____   Date_____

3. Write out your testimony of when you were saved and share it with someone this week.

   x_____   Date_____

The Steps of a Good Man

In these pages we have seen God's definition of a "good man." We have studied nine biblical commitments that a good man will make. Would you consider them as we draw this study to a close?

First, let me ask you some pointed questions: Do you desire to be a good man? When your life is finished and others speak of your living, do you want them to say, "He was a good man"? I believe you do. I believe deep within your heart you long to be a good man—by God's definition.

Perhaps the devil has shamed you over bad decisions, past failures, or present struggles. Perhaps your own heart condemns you, and you feel that you could never measure up to these principles.

As we finish this book, I simply want to remind you that your Heavenly Father desires to create these qualities in you by His power—not by your own. If you feel that you simply cannot fulfill these commitments and character traits on your own, you are right.

But God doesn't expect you to fulfill them alone. He expects you to make these commitments by faith and then to cast yourself in utter dependence upon His daily strength and grace.

When you struggle and fall, He expects you to confess it and to get back up. When you are discouraged, He expects you to wait upon renewed strength from Him. When you are frustrated, He expects you to patiently persist. When you are burdened and tested, He expects you to endure. He calls you to fight "the good fight of faith." He calls you to resist your enemy, to love your wife, to nurture your children, and to honor Him in your living!

On the next page you will find the nine commitments listed once again. Take a moment before you close this book and make a covenant with your God—your Heavenly Father. Pray something like this:

"Father, I truly desire to be a good man by your grace. Today I commit to You that for the rest of my journey through this life I will depend upon You, walk with You, and embrace Your plan for my life. You will be my God, my Father, my daily strength and refuge. You will be my guide and my fortress. I will depend upon You, love You, serve You, and live each day for Your glory. I will love my family, be faithful to my church, resist my enemy, and walk faithfully. When I fail, I will get back up and claim Your grace. When I succeed, I will recognize Your goodness and give You the credit. I ask You to let Your work begin— make me the man You created me to be!"

May God bless you on your journey to become "a good man"!

THE NINE COMMITMENTS OF
A Good Man

COMMITMENT #1
I will walk with God daily in prayer.

COMMITMENT #2
I will seek the daily filling of the Holy Spirit.

COMMITMENT # 3
I will study God's Word daily.

COMMITMENT #4
I will be faithful to a Bible-believing, fundamental, local church.

COMMITMENT # 5
I will be faithful to my wife.

COMMITMENT # 6
I will nurture my children for God.

COMMITMENT #7
I will maintain moral purity.

COMMITMENT #8
I will live separated from the world.

COMMITMENT #9
I will reach other men for Jesus Christ.

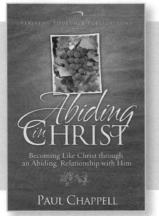

Abiding in Christ

In these pages, Dr. Paul Chappell will lead you on an exciting and encouraging journey to discover the authentic Christian life. You will find the source of true love, abundant joy, lasting fruit, spiritual maturity, emotional stability, and purpose in life. (168 Pages, Paperback)

Ten Principles for Biblical Living

Drawing from over fifty-two years of ministry experience and a profound impact on worldwide missions, Dr. Don Sisk shares ten biblical and practical principles that have shaped his life and ministry. These principles will call you to a renewed life of service for Jesus Christ and are perfect for sharing with others as well. (120 Pages, Hardback)

Grace for Godly Living

In these pages, you will discover that God's grace at work in your life will not only compel you to live a godly lifestyle, but it will give you a spiritual maturity and humility towards those who do not. (160 Pages, Hardback)

done.

Specifically created to be placed into the hands of an unsaved person and a perfect gift for first-time church visitors, this new mini book explains the Gospel in crystal clear terms. The reader will journey step by step through biblical reasoning that concludes at the Cross and a moment of decision. This tool will empower your whole church family to share the Gospel with anyone! (100 Pages, Mini Paperback)

A Faith Full Marriage

Discover how faith should be the foundation and the source of joy and happiness in your marriage relationship. Faith is where God's touch enters the picture—and more than anything, your marriage needs His touch! (104 Pages, Mini Paperback)

Basics of Biblical Parenting

In a culture of disintegrating families, this book provides a clear vision of God's original design for the Christian home. These pages cut straight to the heart and explore the three most important needs of your family and how to meet them by God's power. (88 Pages, Mini Paperback)

Visit us online

strivingtogether.com

dailyintheword.org

wcbc.edu

lancasterbaptist.org